WOMEN IN SOUTHERN AFRICA

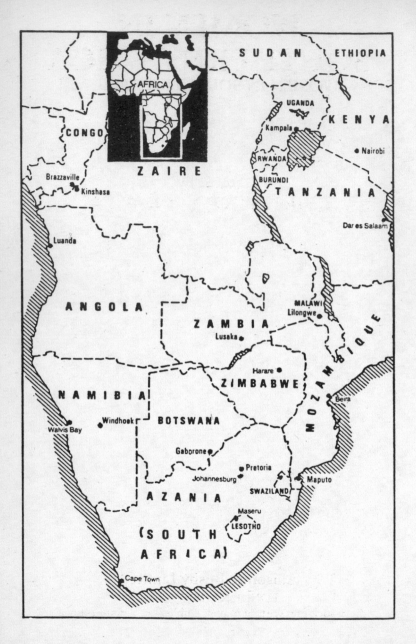

WOMEN IN SOUTHERN AFRICA

edited by
CHRISTINE N. QUNTA

Allison & Busby Limited
LONDON · NEW YORK
(in association with Skotaville Publishers, Johannesburg)

First published in 1987 by
Allison and Busby Limited,
6a Noel Street, London W1V 3RB
and distributed in the USA by
Schocken Books Inc.,
62 Cooper Square, New York, NY 10003.

Copyright © 1987 by Christine N. Qunta and individual authors
All rights reserved

British Library Cataloguing in Publication Data:

Women in Southern Africa.
1. Women, Black——Afirca, Southern——
Social conditions
I. Qunta, Christine N.
305.4'88968   HQ1800

ISBN 0-85031-745-2
ISBN 0-85031-746-0 Pbk

Set in 10/12pt Palatino by
AKM Associates (UK) Limited, Southall, London.
Printed in Great Britain by Billing & Sons Ltd, Worcester

Contents

Dedication

This book is dedicated to the late Amy Jacques-Garvey, who preserved and edited for us and future generations the writings of The Right Excellent Marcus Mosiah Garvey, one of the greatest Africans who lived this century, and to my two daughters, Nehanda and Nzinga, who I hope will grow up and fulfil their potential in a free Azania.

Acknowledgements

I started working on this collection in Australia, far away from Africa, and there were times when things were very difficult. I was sustained during this period greatly by my dear friends and compatriots Vijay and Julia Magan, who, convinced about the need for the book, lent their support and encouraged me. For this I would like to thank them. I would also like to thank Maggie Matlhabaphiri, who typed the first part of the manuscript; Lucky Malete, who typed the last part of the manuscript; Moetaselemo Mosweu for being helpful in so many ways and my husband who proof-read the manuscript and provided a positive intellectual and emotional environment.

Abbreviations

ANC	African National Congress
AZANYU	Azania National Youth Unity
APLA	Azania People's Liberation Army
AZAPO	Azanian People's Organization
AZASM	Azanian Students' Movement
BCW	Botswana Council of Women
BEDU	Botswana Enterprises Development Unit
BOPA	Botswana Press Agency
BOSS	Bureau of State Security
BWU	Black Women Unite
ICJ	International Court of Justice
MPC	Multi-Party Conference
OMA	Organization of Angolan Women
OMM	Organization of Mozambique Women
OPO	Ovamboland People's Organization
PAC	Pan-Africanist Congress of Azania
PANA	Pan-African News Agency
PLAN	People's Liberation Army of Namibia
SADCC	Southern African Development Cooridnating Conference
SASM	South African Students' Movement
SASO	South African Students' Organizations
SSRC	Soweto Students' Representative Council
SWANU	South West Africa National Union
SWAPO	South-West Africa People's Organization
TANU	Tanganyika African National Union
UNIP	United National Independence Party
UNITA	Union for Total Independence of Angola
UTP	United Tanganyika party
UWT	Umoja wa Wamawake wa Tanganyika/Union of Women of Tanganyika
YWCA	Young Women's Christian Association
ZANLA	Zimbabwe African National Liberation Army
ZANU-PF	Zimbabwe African National Union (Patriotic Front)
ZAPU	Zimbabwe African People's Union

9

Preface

African womanhood has been an increasingly topical subject for writers in recent years. Unfortunately, however, the majority of them have not themselves belonged to the community of African women. This in itself is problematic, since the non-African who studies this rather complex issue is inevitably an observer rather than a participant. The limitation is further complicated by the fact that European authors tend to employ theoretical assumptions and a methodology which hamper or in some cases preclude a realistic assessment of the subject-matter.

As a result, the African woman emerges as a victim of the African male and of traditional customs and practices, with colonization playing only a minor role, if any. The African woman of the rural areas is portrayed as little more than a slave, who goes about her tasks with silent acceptance. She has no past and no future, given the inherent backwardness of her society. Her consciousness about her oppression is awakened only when she comes into contact with Western women, and she is surprised by their comparative freedom. She never speaks for herself but is always spoken about. This image is projected with such consistency that it has almost been transformed into "fact" by mere repetition. In part this notion extends to Africans as a race, so that African women come to be perceived in this way not because they are women but because they constitute a section of an oppressed race.

I take the view that we are Africans before we are women, and that the problems we confront in our continent arise largely from the fact that for between a hundred and five hundred years our land and our lives have been ruled by outsiders for their own benefit. Hence, after they have used the minerals, the timber, the agricultural resources and the labour of Africans and grown rich, Africa is left as the continent with the largest number of people unable to feed themselves and with limited access to medical assistance. We lack proper housing and our children are afflicted with preventable illnesses. Even the dissemination of information about health care and other skills is hampered because the majority of our people cannot read and communication networks are inadequate. This situation, in conjunction with a variety of practices which restrict women's access to resources, training and productive employment, conspires to place African women at the bottom of the scale of humanity.

In view of the above, the need to examine the colonization and enslavement of black people is crucial to a study of any aspect of Africa and its people. Slavery has at one time or another been practised by and on most communities in the world. The contrast between the dignity and status of women in early African society and their degradation when slavery took on a racist character, after the end of the mass enslavement of whites, brings to the fore issues which must be closely analysed if we are to understand more clearly some of the perceptions of us perpetuated in literature of the West.

One of the more significant contributions that white scholars and interest groups have made to the illogical notion of European superiority is to blot out the historical achievements of black people. Thus Africans – who invented writing,*

*The Egyptians invented hieroglyphic writing in prehistory, i.e. prior to 3200 BC, and it is the oldest known system of writing (see G. Mokhtar's introduction to Unesco's *General History of Africa*, Vol.II, p.15). Three main scripts can be distinguished: hieroglyphics, dating from prehistory to about 3000 BC; hieratic, dating from the first dynasty (3100 BC–2890 BC) to 200 BC, which was a type of shorthand used mainly by priests; demotic, a much faster, cursive script that developed shortly before 600 BC and replaced hieratic, which continued to be used by the priests (*Encyclopaedia Britannica*, Vol. V, p.913). The Egyptians taught writing to all the peoples they colonized, in particular the Phoenicians, who later carried it to Greece and throughout the Mediterranean in alphabetical form (Cheikh Anta Diop, *The African Origin of Civilization*, Westport, Conn., 1974, p.293).

12

who were the first brick- and stonemasons and whose mathematical genius and architectural skills enabled them to construct marvels such as the Great Pyramid of Giza (for over four thousand years the world's tallest building) and the city of Great Zimbabwe; who between the tenth and fifteenth centuries established the University of Sankore at Timbuktu in the West African Kingdom of Songhay (in present-day Mali) as one of the centres of learning for the whole region, with faculties of Medicine, Law, Grammar, Geography and Art – are today portrayed as a people with no history of civilization before European conquest.

The black writer and researcher should not fall into this racist trap, but should recognize, as Dabi Nkululeko points out later in this book, "that one of the major fronts in the war against colonialism is writing our own history". This fundamental principle is often overlooked by Western scholars, including feminists.

African women must speak for themselves. They should also decide for themselves who they are, where they are going, what obstacles face them and how to remove these. Acknowledgement of this will signal European women's willingness critically to inspect the role their own societies have played and are still playing in the oppression of African people in general and African women in particular; this will allow them to play a supporting role where necessary.

Doing this is not easy, as African women in the diaspora, particularly in Great Britain and in the United States of America, know. They, much more than their continental sisters, have for years been involved in a debate about whether female or black liberation should enjoy priority. The legacy of their violent and forced transportation from their original homeland to the Americas remains. By contrast, white women in the USA and Britain across the class structure occupy a privileged position vis à vis African men and women of whatever class – in terms of the economic and political power they wield, their access to education, health and social services, and the way they are treated by the various instruments of the state such as the police, army and prison force. Black women argue that, in the main, their priorities are different from those of white feminists. When, in the United States, for example, an alarming proportion of the male black population is languishing in jail, with a large number unemployed, it does not seem logical to lay the blame for social, political and economic problems on those men who, like the black women themselves, are victims of an exploitative system. The decision to work within their communities to fight racism is not a choice of options so much as a course of action dictated by circumstances. This does not, however, mean that black women ignore the negative attitudes and practices they may find in their brothers.

The feminist movement itself should be seen in context. It is a reformist rather than revolutionary movement in the West, initiated and sustained by middle-class women of European origin. It has raised the consciousness of these women and played an important role in changing their position for the better. Nevertheless, true emancipation of women goes beyond legislating for equality. If one examines the situation in some West European societies, particularly Sweden and other Scandinavian countries with Social Democratic welfare state arrangements, where women have gone a substantial way toward gaining legal equality, one immediately notices that women continue to be degraded through the portrayal of their bodies as vulgar toys in the pornography that abounds in those same societies.

Furthermore, the careers which carry the most prestige and highest financial rewards are still dominated by male employees, far out of proportion to their numbers in the population. At the United Nations End of Decade for Women conference in Nairobi in 1985 I noticed that several countries sent men either to head their delegation or act as advisers. This was especially obvious at the crucial closed sessions dealing with "contentious" issues such as Zionism and sanctions against South Africa. Maureen Reagan, who officially headed the US delegation, appeared on the first day and on the next flew off to a game park to watch wild animals; cynically, a Negro (the word is used deliberately here) man was relied on to negotiate for America on critical issues. I was never sure whether to laugh or cry. Britain, Sweden and the Soviet Union all sent men to these sessions; as well as being incongruous, it proved to be quite revealing.

The enemies of African women, particularly in Southern Africa, are colonialism and imperialism, white racism, class oppression and sexual oppression. The first step towards true emancipation must be the defeat of colonialism, neo-colonialism and imperialism. The next step is to eradicate all the effects of exploitation based on race, nationality, class and sex. This will come about through the critical examination of all political, economic, religious, educational and cultural institutions, together with the education and organization of the affected communities in an effort to wrest control of our lives from outsiders by whatever means. Only then can we build communities where every adult can at least read and write, where everyone can have access to clean water and adequate food supplies, safe housing, preventative health care and the chance to earn a living.

It is a daunting task, given the present state of the African continent. Hence, as women we cannot afford to be frivolous or divisive; we need to harness the energies of both men and women. This is not to say that we take no account of the patriarchal tendencies that hinder women from making a meaningful contribution to society and leading dignified lives. Such tendencies must be fought at all levels, and I believe this confrontation should take the form of consultation, co-operation and criticism. A good example of how this can work exists in the liberation movements in Southern Africa and the legislation of various enlightened governments in the region. It is sometimes the case that while organizations have literature and policies which contain glowing ideals about eliminating discrimination and obstacles that impede the progress of women, some of the men only pay lip service to these principles, making no positive contribution towards the process and occasionally actively holding up the advancement of the women around them.

If men in the popular movements are party to resolutions about alleviating the oppression of women, they cannot then avoid the inconvenience of sharing or collectivizing domestic chores and child-rearing, the practical side of giving the women more time to catch up with the experience and level of awareness that men have had the opportunity to acquire. The movements have the task of persuading their men to desist from all philistine attitudes, or of coercing them through disciplinary measures if persuasion fails.

This book was prompted by my concern at the dearth of literature by, for and about African women on issues they themselves saw as important.

Through these essays, interviews and biographies, I wanted to give some of the women an opportunity to speak, uncurbed, in their own voices. Many of the papers were originally prepared for forums which dealt with specific issues, and I selected those on aspects I wished to highlight. To illustrate some of the reasons for our virtual absence from the field of research and the difficulties faced by the few who try to change this, I invited Dabi Nkululeko to present a paper on the self-determination of African women in research, using Azania as an example. In the process, her excellent study very clearly defines self-determination for an oppressed nation, the exact nature of the oppression suffered by women in countries such as Azania and the relationship between white settler women and indigenous African women.

On the whole, the contents of this book are intended to reflect the contributions African women have made to the world, as well as what the world has done to black women, particularly those of Southern Africa.

Southern Africa has the last two colonies on the continent: Namibia and Azania (the African name for South Africa). With the assistance of her Western allies, South Africa presents a major threat to peace and development in the area;

even those countries which are politically independent are faced with aggression from the Pretoria regime. Forces of reaction and fascism are locked in battle with forces of liberation and progress. Against this background, the strengths and resourcefulness of women, and also the immense problems they face, are amplified. It is for this reason that the collection focuses on the region.

Accessibility of information has meant that all the contributions deal with countries where English is used as a second language. The countries included have been chosen to represent different phases of the struggle for political and economic independence. Namibia is still under colonial rule and Azania under settler-colonial rule. Botswana and Tanzania, which both gained independence without the need for armed struggle, albeit by different routes, are trying to couple political independence with economic independence. Tanzania, while being geographically in East Africa, has always politically been considered part of the south, mainly because of its major role in supporting both morally and physically the struggles of the region; it is a member of the Southern Africa Development Co-ordinating Conference (SADCC) and a frontline state. Zimbabwe, as the region's first "English-speaking" country to fight a bitter war against a formidable and ruthless enemy and win it, was a natural choice.

Although at first glance the topics might appear diverse, they are interconnected. From my perception of the issues facing women, I wished to elaborate on my interpretation of how the Woman Question fits into the perspective that all people must have self-expression and self-determination. I wanted, then, in this collection not so much a sterile, repetitive account of the problems faced by women *per se*. Rather, I aimed to present an integrated picture of the African woman. She, as a member of her community, should sketch out her society, pose her problem and its origin as well as its solution, whether dealing with the liberation movement in Namibia and Azania, the issue of under-representation of women in local authorities in Zimbabwe, the function of women's organizations in the region or female-headed households in Botswana.

The themes running through the collection may be summarized as follows:

1. The status of women in pre-colonial African societies, particularly during antiquity, was markedly different from what it is now. In my essay I examine the various phases of the continent and the position of women during these phases, within the limits of the information available. Engels's treatise on women and the family is discussed alongside that of the eminent Senegalese historian Professor Cheikh Anta Diop, who reaches a different conclusion from Engels with regard to them. The rest of the essay comprises biographical sketches of influential women over the past 3,500 years, concentrating on their role in decision-making in societies they led. It is intended that it should serve as an overview, a background against which what follows can be viewed, and as such provides a historical continuum. This is what is usually lacking in writings on black women.

2. The main enemies of black women are (with some variation of emphasis in different countries) colonialism and imperialism; racism, class and sex oppression.

3. The solution of their problems is inextricably linked to the destruction of colonial and imperialist domination in the Southern Africa region. With regard to this, their participation is not only desirable but essential.

My intention was to represent each country with an essay, an interview and a biography. This has not proved possible, due to availability and the constraints of time and finance. I have, however, ensured that each country featured (with the exception of Tanzania) has at least two of the above three items; Azania, on account of its topicality, has one extra item.

More research must be done by women on the African continent as well as in the diaspora. Issues such as the position of women in pre-colonial days need closer scrutiny, for colonial practices and laws are often thought to be part of African tradition simply because they have been with us for hundreds of years. When we consider that the influence of foreign religions such as Islam and Christianity has been with Africa for approximately 800 and 500 years respectively – long before formal colonization – the line between indigenous practices and assimilated foreign ones sometimes becomes blurred. Also, I hope other women of Africa will compile a more comprehensive work taking in French- and Portuguese-speaking African countries as well.

Christine N. Qunta
Gaborone, Botswana, 1986

I: General

Outstanding African Women,
1500 BC–1900 AD

Christine N. Qunta

Africa, the birthplace of humanity,[1] has nurtured some of the most advanced civilizations – not simply the well documented ones of Egypt and Ethiopia but others throughout the whole of the continent. Several kingdoms, such as Mwene Mutapa and Songhay, flourished in South, Central and West Africa and developed the arts, advanced science and the mining of metals and precious stones. Even when these levels of development are (often reluctantly) acknowledged by European scholars, there is likely to be a lack of awareness about the prominence which African women achieved in matters of state.

The recorded involvement of African women in state administration and military defence planning dates back about four thousand years, to the civilian rule in Egypt of Nebet during the Old Kingdom (c. 3100 BC–2345 BC). It must be mentioned that the view propagated by European historians that the Ancient Egyptians were not African has been systematically and scientifically laid to rest, thanks to the painstaking research undertaken by African historians; when recording history they sometimes start with Egypt and Ethiopia, where the monuments and testaments of African civilization stand immutable for all to see.

Contrary to the more popularly held view, African women on a continent-wide scale enjoyed great freedom and had both a legal and social equality which, among other things, enabled them to become effective heads of state and military strategists. This essay will attempt to highlight some of their outstanding achievements within the context of their social, economic and political milieu, throughout the various periods of antiquity, slavery, colonialism and so on which the continent experienced.

The first part will deal with the phases Africa passed through and the position of women during antiquity, the second millennium empire-building, the transatlantic slave trade, colonialism and the anti-colonial struggle. In order to provide a theoretical framework, Engels's theory of the origin of women's oppression is examined alongside that of the late Professor Cheikh Anta Diop. The latter argues very persuasively that Engels's formulation is based on incomplete research material, and cannot be applied without qualification to the African woman and family. Matriarchy, Diop concludes, has always been the dominant social system in Africa, modified and changed by external factors rather than an internal evolution as Engels suggests. It is also shown how, with the imposition of foreign religions such as Islam and Christianity coupled with the European onslaught on African values, institutions and morality, the African woman found herself deprived of her position of equality, prominence and respect.

The second part of the chapter contains biographies of some notable African women who, through their contributions to their societies, distinguished themselves as leaders in their own right.

Antiquity

Egypt and Ethiopia

The African, and original, name for Egypt was Khem or Khemit, and was used in reference to its black inhabitants. When the Greeks arrived they mistakenly referred to the whole country by the second name of the city of Menes (also called Memphis), named after the African monarch, King Menes, who initiated the establishment of Egypt's first dynasty. The city's second name was in fact Hikuptah but the Greeks mispronounced it as "Aigyptos", which evolved into Egypt.[2]

Egypt, then, did not exist as a separate state but as the north-eastern region of the vast empire of Ethiopia. The known history of ancient Egypt can be traced to earlier than 4500 BC. Records and carbon-dating are the main sources of authority on the era. For the sake of brevity, however, this essay will deal with only the dynastic period of Egyptian history, the period starting around 3100 BC. This was about the time of the building of the city of Menes, one of the main centres of African civilization.

The Old Kingdom (3100 BC–2345 BC)

This period generally refers to the first five dynasties of Egypt. King Menes, one of the greatest rulers of antiquity, basically set up the dynastic system. He

> brought about the kind of stability and innovations in administration that not only provided a solid foundation for a first dynasty, but also the economic and social conditions necessary for the more uniform expansion of religion, the arts, crafts and the mathematical sciences.[3]

The other great leaders during this period included Athothes Peribsen, Khasekhem, Imhotep, Zoser, Sneferu, Khufu and Khafre, who had the Great Sphinx built in his image. This period also set the pace for some of the most amazing achievements the ancient world was to witness. We know from Herodotus, the "father of History", that ancient Greek scholars often made reference to completing their education in Ethiopia; they and the Asians from the Mediterranean were in awe of the achievements of these Africans.

> According to the unanimous testimony of the Ancients, first the Ethiopians and then the Egyptians created and raised to an extraordinary stage of development all

25

elements of civilization, while other cities, including European and Asians of the near East, were still deep in barbarism.[4]

Professor Diop, who makes this assertion, believes that the explanation for it lies in the favourable Nile River environment, which provided an abundance of water, food crops, fish and game.

During this remarkable period, Pharaoh Zoser introduced carved stone architecture; the fourth dynasty pharaohs built the great pyramids of Giza and also ensured that their undeniably African features were immortalized in statuary form in and around their tombs. Other hallmarks include: the centralization of the administration; the existence of a very powerful clergy sustained by the commanding position religion held in society; labour specialization on the basis of craft or vocation; and a clear-cut division between urban and rural areas, which were major centres of trade with the Eastern Mediterranean. Cyril Aldred,[5] in a book that concentrates mainly on minerals and jewellery, points to a high level of skill in the working of gold during the fourth dynasty, although silver was neither abundant nor as yet properly identified as a separate element; he also speculates about Egypt having been the first home of gold smelting.[6]

The Old Kingdom ended with an uprising by the poverty-stricken unemployed masses against the monarch and nobility during the sixth dynasty. This was the first such upheaval in Egyptian history. Among the factors which gave rise to this were the economic strains caused by the vast bureaucracy and the absolution of the monarchy.

The Middle Kingdom (c. 2300 BC–1370 BC)

This second cycle of Egyptian history covers the period from the sixth to the twentieth dynasty. Known as the Middle Kingdom, it was a period of development from the foundations laid in the Old Kingdom.

A feature of this period was the frequent attempts by

whites from parts of the Mediterranean, who envied Egypt's wealth, to invade and conquer the land. They were sometimes assisted by branded white slaves, whom the Egyptians had captured in victories over the Europeans and Asians of the region. One such successful invasion was by an Asian grouping called the Hyksos, who during the period 1730 BC–1580 BC occupied the eastern region of the Nile delta. The Hyksos were defeated and expelled in 1580 BC and Egypt was restored to a unified independent country.

This restoration was followed by the inception of the eighteenth dynasty, which is generally regarded by historians as one of the golden periods of African development. Much credit for this goes to Queen Hatshepsut, a remarkable woman whose biography is outlined later in this essay. Her successor, Thutmosis III, ruled Egypt at its zenith as the world's leading technical, military and imperial power, conquering all the states of Western Asia and the islands of the Eastern Mediterranean. Among these states were Mitlanni on the Upper Euphrates, Babylonia, Cicilia, Cyprus and Crete. The states of Syria and Palestine were integrated into the Egyptian kingdom[7] and were compelled to pay annual tribute to their African conquerors. During later dynasties, Egyptians took as hostages the sons of the rulers of their satellite states, educating them in the Pharaoh's court with the intention that they would later rule their own countries as good underlings.

Diop regards this as "one of the several causes for the extensive, profound and almost exclusively Egyptian influence on Western Asia and the Mediterranean".[8] He enumerates the following features of Egyptian society during the Middle Kingdom: administrative centralization; merit selection for occupancy of administrative posts; land ownership vested in the Pharaoh, with enough access and control available for the population to use land economically and to sell and alienate their rights in it; the non-existence of a servile labour force except the largely Indo-European slave population. In other words, the indigenous Africans had freedom of movement and the option of working where they pleased, be it in the country or in the cities. The state had ultimate responsibility for organizing production and ensuring the maximum yield from the soil.

Basil Davidson observes a balance between the "security and peace" which the peasants of the Nile enjoyed and the burdens of taxation which the state imposed on their harvest during this period.[9] The scales seem to have been tipped against the interests of the peasants towards the end of the Middle Kingdom. The crisis was two-fold. Internally, the clergy and the bureaucracy were wrangling over the resources from the hard-pressed populace. This created tensions. The monarchy had become absolute, and the clergy desired a restoration of the authority they had enjoyed in the sixth dynasty. As central authority was weakened by these disputes, the Syrian, Palestinian and other slaves rebelled. Externally, various European and Asian powers were preparing to invade the Empire. Some internal reforms appear to have halted the slide and Pharaoh Rameses III was able to beat back the offensive and in the process take many prisoners as slaves. Egypt fell deeper into feudalistic conflicts and upheavals, which resulted in social disintegration.

The Third Cycle: Twentieth to Twenty-fifth Dynasty (1090 BC–661 BC)
The turmoil which governed Egypt lasted for three centuries. It was halted by the re-establishment of a centralized authority which was initiated by the kings of the twenty-fifth dynasty. These were able to re-unify the country and gain the allegiance of the people of all the regions. The Sudanese king Piankhi and the clergy mounted a campaign which defeated a coalition of white rebel former slaves and Indo-European invaders. Despite this success, Egypt was never to enjoy peace and prosperity in its old undivided form. Wars of attrition leading to the capture of the city of Thebes in 661 BC signalled the end of the twenty-fifth dynasty, and ultimately the decline of black political supremacy in the region. Egypt gradually came under the domination of the Greeks, Romans and Persians. The last external power to seize and consolidate

authority in the area, fourteen hundred years later, were the Arabs, who converted the entire Sahel into a Muslim region.

The Position of Women in Egypt

Indigenous Egyptian society was characterized by a strong matriarchy. As in many other parts of Africa, women played a central role in agriculture and their economic contribution was therefore greater than in nomadic hunting and pastoral societies. Some historians argue that women may, in fact, have "discovered" agriculture in prehistoric times. The legend of Osiris and Isis, the Egyptian god and goddess of fertility, lends credence to this view. Isis was the wife and sister of Osiris (marriage between siblings was normal in Egyptian royal circles, serving to curtail succession disputes), and she was also the goddess of corn, being said to have invented it. At harvest time, elaborate ceremonies were performed to honour her as "the creator of all green things".[10]

Monogamy was the prevalent form of marriage with the population. Royalty and court dignitaries practised polygamy in varying degrees, depending on wealth and status. Political and economic rights were transmitted through the woman, who was seen as the more stable element within the family. Even in a sedentary lifestyle, the men appear to have retained a certain nomadism and were more susceptible to travel and migration. The women, on the other hand, tended to raise and feed children and were more inclined to stay put. In every extended family, the females inherited the wealth; on marriage the man brought a dowry to the woman.

No restriction barred Egyptian women from participating in the public affairs of society. Besides the opportunity to reign as monarchs in their own right accorded to royal women, commoners were also able to excel based on merit. The first female non-royal ruler of any country was Nebet. She was prime minister during the Old Kingdom, second in command to King Pepi I, and died four thousand years ago.[11]

AD Second Millennium Empire-Building

Although the foregoing concentrates on the historical background of Northern Africa, this is not to say that the rest of the continent meanwhile stagnated. Great strides were made in other parts in science, architecture, agriculture and the arts, notably in the West African empire which occupied roughly the same situation as (and gave its name to) present-day Ghana. Its actual history goes far back, beyond its known record; on the basis of that record, however, which lists forty-four kings before the Christian era, Ghana's human history can be traced beyond the twenty-fifth dynasty, when the last black pharaohs ruled Egypt (seventh century BC).[12]

This West African empire had vast reserves of gold, which it exported to Europe and Asia. This, and its thousand-year-old expertise in iron smelting and manufacture, accounted for its greatness. In terms of agriculture, wheat, millet, cotton, corn and yams were cultivated. In the iron industry, mining and numerous crafts were organized as guilds: for example, blacksmiths, goldsmiths, stonemasons, brickmasons, water diviners, carpenters, weavers, sandal-makers, potters, etc. Imports from other African countries and abroad in general were salt, textiles, cowrie shells, brass, dates, figs, pearls, fruit, sugar and honey. Exports included gold, ivory and rubber.

The world-renowned University of Sankore in Timbuktu was one of the three principal centres of learning in the West African region.

The Empire of Mwene Mutapa

The empire of Mwene Mutapa in the Southern African region prospered for a long time after the empires to the north had declined. It stretched from above the Zambezi River, including the area of modern Zimbabwe, westward over Mozambique to the Indian Ocean and southward into the Transvaal, below the Limpopo River.

Since the archaeological evidence gathered all over this vast territory makes it clear that iron technology and allied crafts were well advanced here long before the Christian era, the spread of economic revolution over Africa by the Iron Age may well have come from this southern centre as well as from Meroe in the northeast. From the period roughly indicated as early as 300 BC, the states which were to form the Empire of Mwene Mutapa were engaged in a wide range of diversified economic activities that led not only to interstate trade but foreign commerce over the Indian Ocean as well.[13]

The several thousand mining sites of so many different kinds – iron, gold, copper, tin – suggest expert prospectors, just as the ruins of nearby temples and other beautifully designed stone structures tell us that there were great Black architects and stone-masons here just as they had been in Black Egypt when the first pyramids were built.[14]

The first Arabs and Europeans to find these temples, which had been deserted ages before, went about wrecking them "on a scale beyond belief".[15] Those that could not be destroyed – such as the remains of the stone city of great Zimbabwe, an outstanding tribute to the architectural skills of the citizens of the empire – have been explained away as the work of Europeans or, when that argument is defeated, beings from outer space.

Women were not excluded from playing a significant role in these African societies. It is said that the great Arab traveller Ibn Battuta, a Muslim, "was appalled at the freedom that women enjoyed in West Africa when he visited Mali in 1352".[16] For a variety of reasons which are outside the scope of this essay – including natural disasters, wars with foreigners and internal disputes – those empires gradually declined, despite having enjoyed more than a thousand years of grandeur and prosperity.

31

The Transatlantic Slave Trade

Clearly, however, the most devastating occurrence, which would finally destroy not only the physical well-being of these states and their people but, more tragically, the self-esteem of many Africans was the slave "trade". For four centuries, Europeans unleashed a relentless campaign of premeditated violence against the African people, on a scale unsurpassed in the history of the human race.

Two preliminary statements regarding slavery need to be made. First, the Arabs preceded the Europeans in the enslavement of Africans, often with the assistance of treacherous African leaders. This "trade" was concentrated in East Africa. The Arabs are also the last to practise this form of slavery: a United Nations fact-finding mission to Mauritania in 1983 discovered that 100,000 black African men, women and children still serve descendants of Arab settlers as slaves. This practice dates back to the eleventh century, when invading Arab Muslims first took black people as labourers and concubines. The last public slave auction was held in Mauritania in 1978, though slaves are still sold behind closed doors. Adults males sell for R177, while "females who can produce more slaves" fetch up to R3550.[17]

The second point to make is that slavery has been practised by peoples both black and white since time immemorial. Africans in ancient Egypt enslaved their war captives; in many instances, the slaves were allowed to integrate into the society of their captors. As recently as the fifteenth century, Whites, Asians and Africans were sold into slavery in Spain, including Jews, Moors, Syrians, Lebanese, Greeks, Russians and even Spaniards.[18] On 25 February 1530 and 13 September 1532, royal decrees were issued in Spain proscribing the importation of any Whites, Moors, Jews or certain (rebellious) Africans as slaves to Spanish colonial territories.[19] The general enslavement of Whites, however, effectively ended in 1250 AD with the revolt of the Mamelukes (white slaves) against their Turkish and Arab masters.[20] From then on, Africa alone

32

became the hunting-ground for the slaverunners, and the word "African" in the minds of Europeans became synonymous with slave, which equalled subhuman.

On the question of how many Africans were removed from the continent by slave ships, Europeans hasten to quote the figure of ten million. The Guyanese historian Walter Rodney summed up the position as follows:

> In order to whitewash the slave trade they find it convenient to start by minimizing the numbers concerned. The truth is that any figure of Africans imported into the Americas is bound to be low, because there were so many smuggling slaves (and withholding data). Nevertheless, if the low figure of 10 million was accepted as a basis for evaluating the impact of slaving on Africa as a whole, the conclusions that could legitimately be drawn would confound those who attempt to make light of the experience of the rape of Africans from 1445–1870.
>
> On any basic figure of Africans landed alive in the Americas, one would have to make several extensions starting with a calculation to cover mortality in transhipment. The Atlantic crossing or "Middle Passage", as it was called by European slavers, was notorious for the number of deaths incurred, averaging in the vicinity of 15 per cent to 20 per cent. There were also numerous deaths in Africa between time of capture and time of embarkation, especially in cases where captives had to travel hundreds of miles to the coast. Most important of all, given that warfare was the principal means of obtaining captives, it is necessary to make some estimate as to the number of people killed and injured so as to extract the millions who were taken alive and sound. The resultant figure would be many times the millions landed alive outside of Africa, and it is that figure which represents the number of Africans directly removed from the population and labour force of Africa because of the establishment of the slave production by Europeans.[21]

Haki Madhubuti's figure of two hundred and fifty million then sounds more realistic than ten million.[22]

But figures alone cannot accurately convey the effects this visitation had on the African people's development up to this day, on the continent as well as in the diaspora. The following passage touches on the other dimensions of this phenomenon:

> We lost the greatest independent thinkers, those who refused to be slaves and chose death for themselves and their families; we lost the scientists, master teachers, doctors, religious leaders and craftsmen and women who were seen as threats because of the knowledge they possessed and wouldn't betray, and because of their potential as leaders or "troublemakers". We lost the men and women whose commitment to their earth was greater than life as a slave and who refused to surrender to the "devils from the West" or the East and went down in battle after battle. We lost the Black women who smothered their babies while giving them milk and these same women quietly in the night stopped their own breathing rather than surrender themselves sexually or mentally to the foreign trespassers or their own brothers who had turned traitors. The Euroasian trade in Afrikan slaves crippled the Black race, and it was meant that we should never rise again.
>
> Our very soul, the spirit of our ancestors, the meaning of our existence and the very purpose of our lives were eaten from us. . . .[23]

African women also fought to survive this holocaust which was to last for centuries to come. During this time, they would not only suffer the trauma of being removed from their motherland, but also be stripped of the dignified position they occupied in their own communities. Most humiliating was their becoming sexual prey to their captors. The slave-runners visited a terrible vengeance on African womanhood. In the Congo the Catholic priests from Portugal, whose mission it was to eradicate the religion of the Africans and substitute their own, were not only among the most active slave traders who owned ships but also had their own harems of enslaved girls euphemistically referred to as "house servants". This is less surprising in view of the fact that the Catholic church endorsed the slave trade through papal bulls issued by Nicholas V (1454) and Calixtus III (1456).[24]

Women were allowed greater freedom presumably because, in the mind of the European, women were weak and harmless. This sometimes gave African women an advantage in fighting the white slave-drivers. However, the slave-drivers soon realized this. Vincent Harding tells of a certain Samuel Waldo, owner of the slave ship *Africa*, which operated out of Boston, who wrote to his captain in 1734: "For your safety as well as mine, You'll have the needfull Guard over your Slaves, and putt not too much confidence in the Women nor Children lest they happen to be Instrumental to your being surprised which might be fatall."[25]

One example of African women's courage, narrated by Dr Harding, occurred on board the English ship *Robert* as it stood off the coast of Sierra Leone in 1721. There were thirty captives on board, among them a man who called himself Captain Tomba, one of the earliest identifiable leaders of the period of struggle against this form of slavery. He, together with several other men and a woman whose name is not known, planned to attack the crew and find their way back to the shore. The woman, because she had greater freedom of movement, was to inform the men of the best time for the attack. When she reported that the time had come, only one of the men was still prepared to join her and Tomba. They proceeded regardless, but because they were only three and the alarm went off accidentally, no sooner had they managed to kill two crew members than they were overwhelmed by others and placed in chains.

The ship's doctor who wrote about the incident stated that in relation to the two male slaves the Europeans decided to "whipp and scarify them only",[26] as they were strong in build and were therefore valuable "chattels". Three other men who had participated in the planning were first forced to eat the heart and liver of one of the whites killed and were then brutally murdered. As for the woman, the doctor reports: "The woman he hoisted up by the Thumbs, whipp'd and slashed her with Knives, before the other Slaves till she died".[27]

It seems clear from the preceding pages, and will become even more evident in the biographies later in this chapter, that African women have a longstanding tradition of freedom, authority and prominence. However, this stands in sharp contrast to their status in society today. The question then is: how has it happened that the African woman's position has been so drastically altered?

Some of the circumstances giving rise to this erosion of the African woman's independence and freedom have already been touched upon – for example, slavery and colonialism. Specific mention should also be made of the sizeable contribution towards this erosion by the imposition of foreign religions such as Christianity and Islam. Their proponents attempted to destroy (and in some cases were successful) the culture and values of the people with whom they came into contact. Where this occurred, women were seen henceforth as weak and in need of the protection of men, and in certain places to be kept away from them, covered from head to toe, a particular man's property not to be viewed by others.

These were not sufficient reasons in themselves for the change in the status of African women, and other theoretical explanations must be at least briefly explored.

Frederick Engels in his historic treatise *The Origin of the Family, Private Property and the State* argues that the exploitation and oppression of women has its origins in the emergence and development of a society stratified along class lines. The inequalities inherent in such a society can in the final analysis be traced to the socio-economic formation prevalent at a particular period in history.

In primitive communalistic society, men and women were

36

equal and a division of labour existed: women managed the household and the rearing of the children, men procured the food and the implements required. What was produced was always necessary for the needs of the community. Property was owned by the community as a whole. This situation was changed with the emergence of different classes in society more or less coinciding with the domestication of animals and the breeding of herds. This "developed a hitherto unsuspected surplus of wealth and created entirely new social relationships".[28] Relations between men and women were altered. In the old communal household, which consisted of numerous couples and their children, the management of the household was as much a socially necessary industry as the provision of food by men.

Now, with the surplus over and above the cost of maintenance, the man responsible for the procuring of the food and implements necessary came to own these. This was the beginning of the dominance of the man, as a result of his physical ability to capture animals. All surplus wealth produced was owned by the man; the woman shared it but never owned it.[29] The woman's task within the household lost its public character. It was no longer the concern of the society; it became a private service.

The wife became the first domestic servant pushed out of participation in social production.[30]

We knew nothing as to how and when this revolution was effected among the civilized people. It falls entirely within prehistoric times. That it was actually affected is more than proved by the abundant traces of mother right which have been collected, especially by Bachofen.[31]

"Mother right" – that is, the reckoning of descent through the female line and the right of inheritance through the female line – up till then prevailed but was overthrown and substituted by "father right".

In summary, then, the thesis may be stated thus: Matriarchy

was, as far back as the human race can be traced, the system prevailing universally. However, with the change in the mode of production, matriarchy was overthrown and patriarchy instituted.

Diop, in his well researched book *The Cultural Unity of Black Africa*, calls into question the theory of a universal transition from matriarchy to patriarchy. He points out, though, that examination of these ideas "is in no way intended as an attack on the principles of Marxism, it is intended only to show that a Marxist has made use, in a theoretical work, of material the soundness of which has not been proved".[32]

In his work Engels used the research of J. Bachofen and Lewis H. Morgan[33] to illustrate the historical development of human society. He also demonstrated the dynamic relationship between the family and the mode of production prevailing at a given time in history.

Of Bachofen's theory Diop has this to say:

> A first important criticism which can be made of the theory of Bachofen is that it makes an important omission which has not been given sufficient prominence. The demonstration of a universal transition from matriarchy is only scientifically acceptable if it can be proved that this internal evolution has definitely taken place among a specific people. Now this condition has never been fulfilled in the works of the author. It has never been possible to determine the existence of a historical period during which the Greeks and the Romans might have lived under matriarchy.[34]

Both Bachofen and Morgan deduced the existence of a matriarchy from their respective areas of research, Bachofen from classical literature and Morgan from systems of consanguinity prevailing among a particular group of native Americans.

For Diop, however, this is not adequate. In fact he goes further:

When it is examined closely, the theory of Bachofen appears to be anti-scientific. It is unlikely that such geographically different cradles as the Eurasian steppes – favourable to nomadic life – and the southern regions of the globe and in particular Africa – favourable to agriculture and a sedentary way of life – could have produced the same type of social organization. This criticism gains in importance if the influence of environment on social and political forms is admitted. In supposing that matriarchy originated in the south and patriarchy in the north, that the former preceded the latter in the Mediterranean basin, and that in Western Asia both systems were superimposed on each other in certain regions, the hypothesis of a universal transition from one to the other ceases to be necessary; the gaps in the different theories disappear and the ensemble of facts can be explained: the status of women, modes of inheritance, dowries, the nature of consanguinity etc.[35]

South here includes black sub-Saharan Africa, Decca, Melanesia and pre-Columbus America. North includes Europe and Asia.

Can Diop, then, put forward a systematic theory which would fill in these gaps? He formulates his views thus:

If it were proved contrary to the generally accepted theory – that instead of a universal transition from matriarchy to patriarchy, humanity has from the beginning been divided into two geographically distinct "cradles", one of which was favourable to the flourishing of matriarchy and the other to that of patriarchy and that these two systems encountered one another and even disputed with each other in different human societies, that in certain places they were superimposed on each other or even existed side by side, then one could begin to clarify one of the obscure points in the history of antiquity.[36]

He proceeds to analyse north and south in terms of the mode of production, social organization, language and mythology to discover whether these disclose the existence of matriarchy or patriarchy, or both.

After a thorough investigation, which includes data from European historians ancient and modern, Diop concludes in relation to the north:

> As far as one can go back into Indo-European history, especially by means of comparative linguistics, only one form of patriarchal family can be found which seems to be common to all tribes before their divisions (Aryans, Greeks, Romans). Verbal expressions relating to nomadic life are common to all these people unlike those terms which concern the political and agricultural way of life.[37]

Their existence was then based on a series of perpetual migrations. Here,

> the economic role of the woman was reduced to a strict minimum, she was only a burden that the man dragged behind him. Outside her function of childbearing, her role in nomadic society is nil. It is from these considerations that a new explanation may be sought for the lot of the woman in Indo-European society. Having a smaller economic value, it is she who must leave her clan to join that of her husband, contrary to the matriarchal custom which demands the opposite. Among the Greeks, the Romans and the Aryans of India, the woman who leaves her own genus (or gens) to join her husband's gens becomes attached to the latter and can no longer inherit from her own.[38]

Even for a long time after the Indo-Europeans established fixed settlements, their women remained cloistered.

> Engels recalls that at best they learnt to spin, to weave, to sew and to read a little; they could only come in contact with other women. They were secluded in the gynaeceum, which formed a separate part of the household, either on an upper floor or at the rear of the main end of the house, to remove them from the view of men and especially from

strangers. They were not allowed to go out without being accompanied by a slave. The making of eunuchs to watch over the women is typically Indo-European and Asiatic.[39]

By contrast in the southern regions, Africa in particular, matriarchy existed on a continent-wide scale. Diop cites evidence of this from Swaziland, Botswana, Ghana, Zimbabwe and the Congo: "Women took part in public life and had the right to vote, they could become queens and enjoyed a legal status equal to that of men."[40] It is because of this equality that African women such as Queen Hatshepsut, Candace, Cleopatra, Aminatu, Yaa Asantewa, Mma Ntatise, Nehanda and many others rose to prominence. It is therefore not surprising that the first country in the world to be ruled by a woman – Queen Hatshepsut, 1500 BC – was in Africa, namely Ethiopia (when what is now called Egypt was still part of the Ethiopian empire). It is, in fact, in Egypt that matriarchy was most lasting and evident, going back thousands of years. Of Egyptian women Diop says:

> The latter, during the entire history of the Egypt of the Pharaohs, enjoyed complete freedom, as opposed to the condition of the segregated Indo-European woman of the classical periods, whether she was a Greek or Roman. No evidence can be found, either in literature or historical records – Egyptian or otherwise – relating to the systematic ill-treatment of Egyptian women by their men. They were respected and went about freely and unveiled, unlike certain Asian women.[41]

Examining the matriarchal system further, Diop finds that in its purest form a child does not inherit from his father but from his maternal uncle; all political rights are transmitted through the mother. The importance of the brother on the mother's side lies in the fact that it is he who aids his sister, is her representative everywhere and if need be takes her defence, rather than this role falling to her husband. The husband, in fact, was considered a stranger to his wife's family, a concept diametrically opposed to that of the Indo-

European.[42] 'Uncle", in certain African languages, means someone who has the right to sell (implying his nephew); that is to say, in the event of being taken prisoner he can ransom himself by giving his nephew in his place.

Furthermore, among southern societies the mother occupies a highly revered position: all that relates to her is sacred; her authority is virtually unlimited. Diop cites the accounts of Arab travellers and writers around 1352 AD, in particular Ibn Battuta and the French historian Delafosse, on their respective experiences. Referring to the Africans, Ibn Battuta notes they "are named after their maternal uncles and not after their father; it is not the sons who inherit from their fathers but the nephews, the sons of the father's sister. I have never met this last custom anywhere else except among the infidels of Malabar, India".[43]

> The Arab writers who have told us of Ghana and Mandinga (Mali) in the Middle Ages have drawn our attention to the fact that, in these states, the succession was transmitted, not from father to son, but from brother to uterine brother, or uncle to nephew (son of sister). According to native traditions it was the Bambara who first, in the Sudan, broke with this practice and it is from this that they derive their name – Ban-ba-ra or Ban-ma-na, meaning separation from the mother – while those among the Ouangara who remained faithful to the old custom, received the name of Manding or Mande – Ma-nding or Ma-nde, meaning "mother child". In our times male kinship or consanguinity persists among the Bambara and has gained the upper hand among the Sarakolle and among part of the Mandingos or Malinke; but many of these latter still only acknowledge female or uterine consanguinity as conferring the right of heritage, and it is the same among most of the Pelus and the Sereres and among a large number of the Black peoples of the Sudan, the coast of Guinea and of Africa south of the Equator.[44]

In Africa this is evident from the respect accorded to the

mother or her relatives. It is believed that how a person conducts himself towards his mother will determine whether or not he will lead a happy, settled life. To behave immodestly or improperly towards one's mother is to be inviting a curse.

Among the Asante (Ashanti) and other Akan peoples of Ghana, descent is also matrilineal. Diop quotes from A.R. Radcliffe-Brown and D. Forde, who wrote in 1953:

> The Ashanti consider the bond between mother and child as the keystone of all social relations.... They consider it as a moral relationship which is absolutely binding.... To show disrespect to a mother is equivalent to committing sacrilege.[45]

The gradual transformation from a matrilineal regime to a patrilineal one Diop ascribes mainly to outside forces, chief among these being foreign religions:

> The African who has been converted to Islam is automatically ruled at least as far as his inheritance is concerned by the patriarchal regime. It is the same with the Christian, whether Protestant or Catholic.[46]

The process was further enhanced by colonial practices and legislation. The Islamization of West Africa, for instance, occurred from the tenth century onwards. The African religions with their accompanying norms and customs were weakened and gradually disappeared under the influence of Islam. It is also from the Arabic influence of Islam that the practice of adopting the father's name (as opposed to the maternal uncle's) seems to have originated. The practice of naming a child after the maternal uncle was still in existence in 1353 when Ibn Battuta visited the region.

Despite these external forces, vestiges of matriarchy still exist. In Azania, for instance, despite the high level of industrialization and a very brutal process of colonization, among black people one's mother occupies a very central and respected place in the family and community. Illtreating one's mother is considered to be the worst sin and invites scorn not only from family but from the community at large.

In the Cape, among the Xhosa-speaking people, the woman retains her family or clan name; the clan supersedes the nuclear family. It is a much older phenomenon than the surname in this region. From one's clan name may be traced several generations of predecessors, as well as elements of the family's history and past achievements.

Among the MaMfengu, the MaGcaleka, the MaRarabe and other Xhosa-speaking peoples, there was no equivalent title for "Mrs Jones". A woman retained her family name and practised the customs of her family throughout marriage and the rest of her life. Ties with her family thus remained very strong. A woman may sometimes also be referred to in terms of her first child – for example, "Naka Nomsa" (mother of Nomsa).

In a study on Swazi royalty[47] we are informed that the queen mother's village is always the capital. She rules with the king and they both have a hereditary title. Between them,

> there is a delicate balance of powers, legal, economic and ritual. He presides over the highest court and formerly he alone could pronounce the death sentence. But she is in charge of the second highest court, her counsellors may take part in discussion at her son's court, and her hut is a sanctuary even for men sentenced to death. . . . He has his own chosen regiments stationed at his home; she has regiments at the capital under the leadership of princes. She is the custodian of the sacred objects of the nation, but they are not effective without his cooperation in manipulating them.[48]

More importantly:

> The fundamental principle underlying the selection of an heir is that power is inherited from men and acquired by them; but it is transmitted through women whose rank more than any other single factor determines the choice of successor. Nkosi Ngunina! (a ruler [is ruled] by his mother).[49]

Diop's criticism of Engels and his conclusion can be summarized as follows: in postulating the existence of a universal matriarchy evolving to a patriarchy, Engels used incomplete material research. Consequently, he has been unable to establish the logical connection permitting the transition from matriarchy to patriarchy and the affirmation of the universality of the process leading from one to the other. Engels's admission that it is not known how and when this took place is further evidence of the fact that the process is merely postulated but that its existence has not been demonstrated.

After a detailed and well documented study of Engels's work, the history, languages, mythologies, norms and religions of Europe, Asia and Africa, Diop argues that instead of a universal transition from matriarchy to patriarchy humanity has always been divided into two distinct cradles, one favourable to patriarchy (for example, Europe) and the other favourable to matriarchy (for example, Africa). In some societies, the two systems met and even co-existed side by side. In Africa, an agricultural and sedentary lifestyle favoured the flourishing of matriarchy, which prevailed throughout the whole continent. Its gradual erosion and subsequent substitution by patriarchy is not, as Engels argues, an internal "natural development" but rather the result of external factors.

Diop's contribution to this important debate renders an uncritical and mechanical acceptance of Engels's theory impossible, especially for those researchers who are interested in unearthing African history as it is, and not as it has been presented to us by the very people who enslaved us physically and mentally. It is, therefore, incumbent upon African researchers interested in the woman question to follow the lead given by historians such as Diop and further explore the thesis of African matriarchy.

Queen Hatshepsut
(15th century BC)

Queen Hatshepsut was, according to the Egyptologist James Henry Breasted, "the first great woman in history of whom we are informed".[50] She ruled Egypt during the eighteenth dynasty, fifteen hundred years before the birth of Christ.

The only child of the Pharaoh Thutmosis I and his queen Ahmosis,[51] Hatshepsut derived from her mother and her grandmother Alchotpou rights of succession over and above those of her husband Thutmosis II and her own father. She ruled first as regent for Thutmosis III, her husband's son by another wife, and then in her own right. Queen Hatshepsut's reign lasted for twenty-two years (c. 1490–68 BC), during which time she established a reputation as one of the most brilliant leaders Egypt had known. Chancellor Williams describes her as the greatest woman Pharaoh of black Egypt; she was "a queen absolute, ruling alone as a king (to emphasize the point she often dressed in royal male attire, including the false beard and wig)".[52]

She organized the first sea expedition to the coastal lands that correspond to present-day Somalia, bringing back varieties of plants which she adapted to Egypt. Under her rule Egypt flourished through the expansion of foreign trade, international diplomatic relations, the streamlining of national defence and increased public building programmes. One of the projects which interested her most was the building of a great navy for the purpose of both commerce and war. Her success in such projects assured her immortality.

The great funerary temple Hatshepsut had built for herself, the tomb of Deir el-Bahri, to this day remains one of the foremost tourist attractions of Egypt.

Queen Candace
(3rd century BC – 2nd century AD)

> When the Indo-European world [Persians, Greeks,
> Assyrians, Romans] acquired enough military strength to
> conquer the old countries [Ethiopia and Egypt] that had
> civilized it, they encountered the fierce, unyielding resis-
> tance of a queen whose determined struggle symbolized
> the national pride of a people who, until then, had
> commanded others.[53]

This is how Diop describes one of the best generals of the
ancient world, Queen Candace, Empress of Ethiopia and
General-in-Chief of its armies. Her courage and tactical ability
made her a legend, such that Sudanese queens later inherited
her name.

Candace reigned during the period when Augustus Caesar
was at the height of his power. After he conquered Egypt,
Alexander drove his Roman armies across the Nubian desert
to the frontiers of Ethiopia. Candace at the head of her troops
waited on the border for the invaders. According to legend,
her reputation was so impressive that Augustus Caesar did
not want his army to encounter her, for fear of losing the
battle at the hands of a woman,[54] so he halted at the borders of
Ethiopia.

Since the notion of a woman playing a political and social
role was for the Indo-Europeans quite unheard of, Queen
Candace was indeed a remarkable phenomenon.

There were other African women of prominence during
antiquity, some well-known such as Nefertiti, who ruled
Egypt in 1365 BC, and the famous Queen of Sheba, sometimes
referred to as Queen Makeda. She ruled Ethiopia in 960 BC and
is mentioned in both the Bible and the Koran. The Greeks
spoke of her as the "Black Minerva".

Queen Cleopatra (c. 69–30 BC)

More nonsense has been written about Cleopatra than about any other African queen, mainly because it has been the desire of many writers to paint her white. She was not a white woman, she was not a Greek. Let us dispose of this matter before explaining the more important aspects of her life. Until the emergence of the doctrine of white superiority Cleopatra was generally pictured as a distinctively African woman, dark in colour. Shakespeare in the opening line of *Anthony and Cleopatra* calls her "tawny". In the Book of Acts, Cleopatra describes herself as black.[55]

The fact that Cleopatra had in her ancestry some Asian blood does not transform her racially into a European. Furthermore, the jewellery and adornments worn by Cleopatra and other ancient Egyptian and Ethiopian women – as depicted in drawings, statues and carvings in tombs, in particular the breastplate and head-dresses – are still worn with great elegance by African women throughout the continent. Examples that immediately come to mind are the people of Masai extraction in East Africa and women along the eastern coast of Azania, who traditionally wear breastplates. These would in the past have been sculpted out of precious metals such as gold and silver but are now made out of seeds and glass beads, the latter introduced to Africa by missionaries and European traders.

Cleopatra in 51 BC shared the throne with her brother Ptolemy XIII and commenced her rule when she was eighteen years old. Egypt at this stage was no longer the pride of its people but had become a Roman protectorate. To strengthen her rule, Cleopatra formed an alliance with Julius Caesar. After Caesar's murder, she met Mark Anthony and pursued a relationship with him. He betrayed Rome on account of Cleopatra, and when he died she committed suicide rather than accept the humiliation of Egypt being totally dominated by the Romans.[56]

Queen Nzinga of Angola and Ndongo
(c. 1581–1663)

One woman who became a legend during her lifetime for her resistance to the Portuguese slave racketeers and colonizers was Queen Nzinga. She was a formidable strategist, which fact the Portuguese, imbued with backward ideas regarding women, found astonishing especially since this one also had a black skin. Born in 1583, she had as a brother Ngola Bbondi, the reigning king of Ndongo (the area now called Angola,[57] since the Portuguese mistook the title of the ruler – *ngola* – for the name of the country).

After rampaging through Angola, the Portuguese decided that it was sufficiently subdued for the final takeover; thus, by their royal decree, Angola became Portugal's colony in 1575.[58] However, the Portuguese had not anticipated having to wait for at least another forty years and fighting a very costly war with the Angolan army, led by an outstanding general in the form of Queen Nzinga of Ndongo.

During his reign Nzinga's brother initially cooperated with the Portuguese and sold his own people into slavery. She opposed him, rallying the Angolan people when he finally began to resist the Portuguese. A war followed in which Portuguese casualties were so high that they were forced to admit defeat. In 1622 Portugal proposed a peace conference held at Luanda. Nzinga was not yet queen but she headed the African delegation, exhibiting her skills as a negotiator at this conference. The terms of the treaty added insult to injury for the Portuguese, as they were obliged to make numerous concessions, including evacuating all their nearby fortifications, and to free all the chiefs who had become vassals of the Portuguese king and restore them to their former status. The most important concession made by Nzinga was to return the Portuguese prisoners-of-war she held. The treaty was meant to end all the fighting but the Portuguese, smarting from their defeat at the conference table, invaded the Kongo.

In 1623, after the death of her brother, Nzinga became queen, and she immediately sent an ultimatum to the Portuguese, demanding that the terms of the treaty be executed forthwith, otherwise war would be declared. It was at this time that the Dutch arrived on the scene with the purpose of ousting the Portuguese in order to loot West and Central Africa of its mineral wealth and enslave its people. The contest for African soil and people between these two European powers gave the queen a chance to plan her strategy.

Nzinga was assured a revered place in history on two counts. First, in 1624 she nominated the whole of Angola a free country and declared that all Africans running away from the slave traders and reaching territory under her control would remain free. Secondly, she undermined the Portuguese policy of using black soldiers against the African people. To this end she carefully selected groups of her own soldiers who would spread out individually into Portuguese-held areas and allow themselves to be recruited. Once they had infiltrated the Portuguese army, then they quietly set about convincing the troops where their true loyalty should lie. So successful was this campaign that whole companies deserted to Queen Nzinga, taking with them much-needed guns and ammunition. Her armies were further strengthened by runaway slaves who came into the free zone she had proclaimed.

Incensed at the boldness of this woman, the Portuguese sent her an ultimatum demanding the immediate return of all chiefs, soldiers and slaves from territory under Portuguese control, or else war would be declared. When these divide-and-rule tactics failed, they arrogantly pronounced that Nzinga was not legally queen of Ndongo and that the throne was therefore vacant. One of their puppet chiefs, Aidi Kiluanji, was declared king.[59] They then prepared an all-out offensive against Nzinga, marshalling their forces on land and sea, but she struck first against the puppet king and his force. When in July 1626 the Portuguese captured her principal island stronghold in the Cuanza River, thus dividing her forces and cutting off main supporting regiments, Nzinga left Angola, whereupon the Portuguese crowned Aidi Kiluanji as King Philip I of Ndongo.

The people's unwavering loyalty to Queen Nzinga, however, was rewarded in November 1627 when, at the head of an army bolstered by loyal chiefs and freed men, she returned to recapture the Cuanza stronghold.[60] The Portuguese retreated and, to avoid the humiliation of having to admit defeat at the hands of an army led by a woman, cited the Dutch presence as an excuse, though in fact no imminent Dutch threat existed.

As the Portuguese were regrouping with the intention of destroying Nzinga once and for all, first offering a big reward for her capture dead or alive, she once more outwitted them by leaving the country while instructing her lieutenants to spread the rumour that she had fled and been killed on mistakenly entering an enemy's territory. The Catholic bishop celebrated a special mass in recognition of this "special blessing"; the Portuguese could at last settle down to colonizing Angola without interruption. But to their astonishment in 1629 Queen Nzinga victoriously re-entered the country, crushing all Portuguese opposition in her path.[61] They were comprehensively defeated.

Queen Nzinga became ruler of Matamba, a neighbouring kingdom. She continued her efforts to stem the evil of slavery and dealt ruthlessly with rulers involved with it. Having no alternative, the Portuguese finally decided to implement the treaty of 1622 and declared Portugal's wars against her unjust. Hostilities, however, did not cease. By 1641 the Dutch had reduced Portugal's influence along the coast. Queen Nzinga's stubborn opposition did not help matters for them. When it suited her, she formed an alliance with the Dutch against the Portuguese, knowing that she would deal with them once the Portuguese were defeated. Finally in 1656, after forty years of war with the Portuguese, outwitting them repeatedly, she signed a treaty in order to rest her strife-torn country, six years after the initial offer of peace from them.

The last seven years of her life were spent consolidating and developing her country's economy, as she was aware that the Portuguese were still entrenched in strategic areas. Queen Nzinga died in 1663, having utterly frustrated Portuguese attempts at colonizing her territory. Her people mourned the passing of their beloved queen, a true patriot in the fullest sense of the word.

Queen Aminatu of Nigeria*
(c. 16th century)

Historians record that the seven states making up the Hausa empire – Daura, Kano, Gobir, Zazzau, Katsina, Rano and Garun Gabas – came into existence around 1050 AD. Before they were established that region of West Africa was ruled by a dynasty of seventeen queens.

Synonymous with the building of a strong and united Hausa empire in the sixteenth century is Queen Aminatu, eldest daughter of Queen Bakwa Turunku of Zazzau. (The state was later renamed Zaria after Queen Turunku's youngest daughter.) The date of Aminatu's becoming queen is estimated to have been around 1536 and she reigned until 1573.

Immediately after starting her reign, Queen Aminatu initiated military campaigns to conquer the neighbouring states. She was a shrewd and skilful leader of her army of twenty thousand men and was in personal command when they conducted campaigns to annex several states, receiving many luxurious gifts from the leaders of these states. She continued her campaigns for an uninterrupted period of thirty-four years; some of the fortifications which she built around her camp still stand today and are named after her.

Trade in the Hausa empire expanded both nationally and internationally during Queen Aminatu's reign, consisting

*This account of Queen Aminatu's life draws on information from *Africa Woman*, No. 33, May/June 1981, and David Sweetman's *Women Leaders in African History* (London: Heinemann, 1984), p. 22.

mainly of goods produced by craftsmen – blacksmiths, weavers, dyers, tanners and leather workers. The Hausa language was used by traders, and Hausa centres became flourishing market towns, with the state of Zaria the focus of the north-south Sahara trade and east-west Sudan trade.

Queen Aminatu died in Atagara, in Gara near present-day Idah. After her death the stature of Zaria was never quite the same, but her military achievements and advances in trade have assured her an elevated place in the history books of Africa. Nigeria immortalized this powerful woman by erecting a life-size statue of her on horseback, sword in hand, in the grounds of the National Theatre in Lagos, and in the northern states there are also many educational institutions named after her.

Queen Mma Ntatise of the BaTlokwa
(c. 1781–1835)

Although not as well known as some of her precursors, Mma Ntatise ranks high on any list of outstanding African women.

At the beginning of the nineteenth century in the Southern Africa region, several communities were warring against one another over territorial claims. One of these groups was the Tlokwa people. Their monarch died leaving an heir who was still a minor, Sekonyela, so his mother, Mma Ntatise, acted as regent.

Her people were caught unawares and were driven from their homes by Hlubis, an Nguni ethnic group from the region of present-day Natal. From then on the Tlokwas, under the leadership of Mma Ntatise, blazed a trail of conquest and subjugation, moving westward to the vicinity of Kurutlele mountain, near the Sand River.[62] Mma Ntatise had a reputation for being ruthless with her enemies and she became one of the most respected and feared leaders of the region. Legend has it that in order to subdue her enemies she deliberately spread rumours to the effect that captives were eaten alive, and by this means her relatively small nation instilled fear in other powers.

The Tlokwa eventually moved in a south-easterly direction to establish a base close to the mountain of Butha-Buthe in the north-west corner of Lesotho.[63] This was right next to the stronghold of Moshoeshoe, the founder-king of Lesotho, whose following was not yet as large as it was later to become. Mma Ntatise attacked his stronghold but did not get very far, though a significant incident occurred at this point. On a counter-attack, Moshoeshoe's forces penetrated the centre of the Tlokwa base and almost destroyed them, but for the bravery of a woman named Meseile. She grabbed one of the fleeing soldiers and berated the Tlokwa for allowing themselves to be routed by an inferior force. Because of her action the course of that war was dramatically changed. Moshoeshoe's men were pushed back to their mountain base and most of their cattle were seized. This particular battle is known as the "Battle of the Pots", because many cooking-pots in the Tlokwa camp were broken.

Mma Ntatise was known to be endowed with a brilliant mind, which accounted for the respect she commanded from friend and foe alike. A clear example of her quick-wittedness can be seen in the following description of an event that took place when Sekonyela had come of age and led the army. While they were stationed at Tlapeneng, the Hlubi sent out a retaliatory expedition to the Tlokwa base, which was virtually undefended as Sekonyela had led the men on an expedition in the vicinity. Faced with an almost hopeless situation Mma Ntatise quickly "formed all the available men into single rank, made the women line up behind them waving the handles of hoes instead of spears and holding up sleeping-mats to look like shields. Faced with what looked like a combat formation, the Hlubi hesitated and as they did so Sekonyela, returning with the fighting men, came upon them and inflicted a severe defeat."[64]

The Tlokwa became a very powerful group and played an important role in the shaping of the history of the region.

Although by 1837 Sekonyela was the effective ruler, his mother continued to be held in great esteem. It is said that when important visitors were received, they would be introduced first to the Queen Mother. ·

Nehanda of Zimbabwe (c. 1862–98)*

Zimbabwe was once part of the mighty and prosperous Mwene Mutapa empire which mined and exported precious metals and pioneered the unique stone architecture in evidence up to this day in Great Zimbabwe, at Masvingo. Much later, with the arrival of the British invaders whose greed and brutality caused the African people untold trauma, there emerged a woman who would become in life and death the single most significant person in the modern history of Zimbabwe. Her name was Nehanda Nyakasikana and she is reverently referred to as Mbuya (Grandmother) Nehanda by Zimbabwean patriots.

Nehanda was born around 1862 in what is now the Chishawasa district of Central Zimbabwe, into a large and religious family. According to Zimbabwean historian Tendai Mutunhu,[65] she exhibited remarkable leadership qualities and organizational skills as she grew up. It was through these attributes that she was able to rise to one of the most influential positions within the religious hierarchy of the MaShona nation. Another factor was her acquisition of an in-depth knowledge of the Shona religious creed and theology.

At the outset of the British invasion of Zimbabwe, Nehanda was one of the country's two most influential religious leaders, the other being a man called Kagubi. Of this invasion, Mutunhu says: "The British colonization of Zimbabwe was accomplished with the financial backing and military support of Africa's greatest racist and most notorious imperialist –

*Material on Nehanda was largely drawn from Tendai Mutunhu's essay "Nehanda of Zimbabwe".

Cecil John Rhodes."[66] In 1889 Rhodes, assisted by a missionary who spoke Ndebele, deceived King Lobengula into signing away the mineral rights of his country, in the so-called Rudd Concession. Armed with this document (which some historians believe may have been forged), Rhodes obtained the permission of Queen Victoria of England to colonize Zimbabwe. In 1890 he recruited two hundred white soldiers from South Africa to spearhead the occupation of Zimbabwe and the operation was financed and equipped by the British South Africa Company, which accumulated millions through its exploitation of African mine workers. The colonizers were each promised a 3,000-acre farm of land of his own choice (land to be forcibly taken from Africans) and fifteen gold claims anywhere in Zimbabwe.

The settlers, on arrival, proceeded to confiscate the Africans' land and cattle. They also subjected Zimbabwean women to sexual abuse, outraging the black people, as they held their women in high esteem. Nehanda opposed the invaders' rule as soon as it was imposed. Observing their behaviour, she believed these white people to be evil, inhuman and destructive, and she saw their presence as the greatest threat to the survival of African social, political, religious and economic institutions.

Not surprisingly for a community where religion and religious activity dominated every aspect of life, the people turned to their religious leaders for guidance when the decision was taken to fight the invaders.[67] Nehanda was one of the first to respond. They informed her of the activities and crimes of the settlers and she, in consultation with Kagubi and other leaders, declared war. They conferred on a meticulously planned strategy. At the head of military operations was the Shona chief priest Mkwati, who at the time resided at Taba Zika Mambo in the Matopo Hills. He strongly urged unity between Shona- and Ndebele-speaking Zimbabweans. The military forces in the south and south-west launched the first "Chimurenga" (liberation) war in 1896, and the rest of the country followed suit in June 1897. Even the whites acknowledged Nehanda's influence and her tactical ability: "At the present moment Nianda [sic] is the most powerful wizard in Mashonaland and has the power of ordering all the people who rose lately and her orders would in every case be obeyed."[68] Shortly before the war started, she established her operational headquarters at Musaka in the Mazowe district.

> Musaka was an impregnable mountain fortress with a network of caves with plenty of water, some stored grain, kraals for cattle, and was inaccessible except through the narrow and dangerous passages. Well armed and trustworthy guards were stationed at all entrances to this mountain fortress. Nehanda was to direct her war effort(s) from Musaka. Her military commanders were two brothers named Chidamba and Chireshe who were to distinguish themselves in battle.[69]

She identified as chief military targets the white settlers, their farms, mines and trading posts, as well as policemen and Africans who collaborated with the invaders. Besides co-ordinating and commanding her forces, Nehanda also gathered intelligence, including establishing the whereabouts of the whites and the movement of their troops, which she then passed on to her soldiers in the field. Her main sources were spies, informers and fire signals. She insisted on strict discipline among her forces. Looting was forbidden, except for weapons to replenish their own stocks. Gunpowder was manufactured from local materials. Missiles were made from lengths of telegraph wire, nails and glass balls from soda-water bottles. Guns were obtained from Dutch settlers or Portuguese gun-traders and African police defectors; some were also stolen from the British. Nehanda is said to have accompanied her soldiers on to the battlefield on occasion, though it is not known if she took part in the actual fighting.

From June to August 1897 the war grew in intensity. The Africans were in complete control of the rural areas, so much so that the British government had to send in reinforcements to bolster the beleaguered settlers. The reinforcements were soon removed, since they proved incapable of improving the settlers' position. From the middle of August the situation changed. The British ended hostilities in the south and south-west by going into negotiations with the Ndebele-speaking population. From that point, they were able to concentrate all their forces against Nehanda's strongholds. Also, while the whites were able to amass fresh stocks of guns, Nehanda's forces were experiencing problems resupplying themselves.

In December that year, Nehanda and Kagubi were captured in the Dande and brought to the then Salisbury in chains and under heavy guard. She was charged with causing and instigating rebellion and with murdering the Native Commissioner, Pollard, notorious for his cruelty. A state witness alleged that she had said, "Kill Pollard, but take him some way off to the river or he will stink."[70] She was tried on 2 March 1898, found guilty and sentenced to death. Kagubi, charged with the murder of an African policeman, was also to be hanged.

Nehanda was executed on 27 April that year. A Catholic priest tried to convert her to his faith but she steadfastly refused to embrace the enemy's religion. She remained fearless and defiant to the very last, demanding to be sent to die with her people. It is said that the first attempts on her life failed and it was only the third that succeeded. The Africans mourned. The whites rejoiced. "Everyone felt relieved after the execution," wrote the white priest, Richartz, who had tried to convert Nehanda, "as the very existence of the main actors in the horrors of the rebellion, though they were secured in prison, made one feel uncomfortable. With their deaths, it was universally felt the rebellion was finished, their bodies were buried in a secret place so that no natives could take away their bodies and claim that their spirit had descended to any other prophetess or witchdoctor. The younger generation, it was hoped, now knew that the white Queen meant to reign."[71]

Yaa Asantewa of the Asante
(c. 1840/60–1921)

The Asante (Ashanti) are one of the peoples with the longest-standing history and traditions in West Africa. Their culture and identity pre-date by hundreds of years their rise as a powerful force and empire to establish dominance over the former overlords of the region, the Denkyira. The soldier king Osei Tutu rallied the Asante around the concept of the sacredness of the Golden Stool of the Asante, which is not, as might be expected, the royal throne but a shrine and revered symbol. Thus, in the 1700s the Asante rose to the position of a great regional power.

Their authority was never seriously threatened until about 150 years later, when the British government assumed the role previously played by British merchant companies in colonizing West Africa. Two factors which worked in favour of the British at the time were the style of conquest employed by the Asante people – they did not completely absorb their conquered neighbours or disperse their armies, which meant the latter could always rebel when circumstances permitted – and the contest for succession during the late mid-nineteenth century, which led to civil war among the states that made up the Asante empire. The British army's most decisive victories over the Asante were in 1874, when for the first time they marched into Kumasi, the capital of Asante territory, and in 1896. It was in 1896 that they were able to force the Asantehene (king) Prempeh I to accept a representative of their governor to reside in Kumasi and exiled the Asantehene and his mother to the Seychelles when he would not pay their various tributes. (His mother would have been the regent, according to Asante law, had she stayed.) The major objective of British conquest was the appropriation of the territory's vast reserves of gold and other resources. It was not for nothing that the place was named the Gold Coast.

When the next king Nana Kuma, a relation of Prempeh I,

ascended the Asante throne, his main adviser and chief counsel was his mother Queen Yaa Asantewa. This situation was neither unique nor accidental.

> The importance of women in Asante government is shown by the fact that a new *asantehene* was selected by the queen mother, in consultation with certain advisers, from among her daughter's sons or her daughter's daughter's sons.[72]

Yaa Asantewa is perhaps one of the few women in history after whom a war which she inspired, planned and led was named. She came from the Oyoko clan in Edweso, about 16 kilometres east of Kumasi in what is now Ghana. From the outset of her reign as queen mother, she agitated against the Asante empire being part of the British protectorate of the Gold Coast. Her opportunity to bring the rebellion to the fore was presented by one Sir Frederick Hodgson, appointed by the British as governor of the "protectorate" in 1900. To his simple way of thought, if the Asante had a Golden Stool then he as representative of the British crown had the prerogative to sit on it; this much he expressed at a meeting with the Asante nobility during a visit to Kumasi. It was a sacrilege on the scale of someone proposing to Muslims the preparation of swine for a barbecue in the Khabaa in Mecca, or a strip-show in St Peter's Basilica in the Vatican to Catholics.

It took three days for the preparations to be made and for the Yaa Asantewa war to begin. The British governor tried to sue for peace when he discovered that plans for hostilities were afoot. He was not, however, able to meet the conditions demanded by the Asante: the return of Prempeh I.

The Asante laid siege to Kumasi, taking a vicious toll of the British and their missions in the fort. The British were forced to mobilize over one thousand troops with new weapons from all over their colonies in Africa. Three months later, they managed to break the siege. At every stage the Asante fought relentlessly, but the British wore down the various patriotic leaders and their forces by attrition and with the most modern weapons of the time.

The initial contingent of 350 soldiers sent to capture the Queen at Edweso met with stiff resistance from the last remaining chiefs and patriots. After their retreat from her stronghold, it took two thousand heavily armed troops to capture Yaa Asantewa and her loyalists. Even in defeat, her struggle to assert Asante dignity seems to have been a success. While she too, like her predecessor, was exiled to the Seychelles, most of her subject chiefs were accorded prisoner-of-war status. After her death some twenty years later, Prempeh I was allowed to return from exile, and in 1935 his son Prempeh II was restored to the position of Asantehene. The spirit of Yaa Asantewa lives on in the praise songs and in the sense of identity of the Asante people.

Notes

1. Notwithstanding the gaps still remaining in piecing together the story of the evolution of humanity, modern historians generally agree that Africa is the cradle of humanity. The late Dr Louis S.B. Leakey, the distinguished British archaeologist, has tended to confirm this by his historic findings in the Olduvai Gorge in Tanzania. His son Richard, who followed in his father's footsteps, says: "It was Darwin who first pointed to Africa as the home of man, and during the past hundred years research has shown how correct he was. (...) There is good evidence to suggest that Africa was the continent on which man first made his appearance and later developed upright, bipedal gait as a component of his technological adaptation." (Richard Leakey, "African Fossil Man", in *Unesco General History of Africa*, Vol. I, ed. J. Ki-Zerbo, 1981, p.437.)
2. Chancellor Williams, *The Destruction of Black Civilization* (Chicago: Third World Press, 1976), p.68.
3. Williams, op. cit., p.67.
4. Cheikh Anta Diop, *The African Origin of Civilization* (Westport, Conn.: Lawrence Hill & Co., 1974), p.230.
5. Cyril Aldred, *Jewels of the Pharaohs* (London: Thames & Hudson, 1971), p.16.
6. Ibid., p.19.
7. Diop, *African Origin*, op. cit., p.209.
8. Ibid.

9. Basil Davidson, *Africa – History of a Continent* (New York: Macmillan, 1972), p.30.

10. Cheikh Anta Diop, *The Cultural Unity of Black Africa* (Chicago: Third World Press, 1978), p.60.

11. An Australian archaeological team excavating in Egypt discovered the tomb of Nebet in 1983, as reported in *The Australian*, November 1983.

12. Williams, op. cit., p.210.

13. Williams, op. cit., p.291.

14. Williams, op. cit., p.293.

15. Ibid.

16. Diop, *Cultural Unity*, op. cit., p.x.

17. Johannesburg *Star*, world and national edition, 15 February 1984.

18. Leslie B. Rout, Jr, *The African Experience in Spanish America* (Cambridge: Cambridge University Press, 1976), p.17.

19. Ibid., p.24.

20. Williams, op. cit., p.81.

21. Walter Rodney, *How Europe Underdeveloped Africa* (London: Bogle-L'Ouverture Publications, 1972), pp.104–5.

22. Haki R. Madhubuti, *Enemies: The Clash of Races* (Chicago: Third World Press, 1978), p.13.

23. Ibid.

24. Rout, op. cit., p.11.

25. Vincent Harding, *There is a River: The Black Struggle for Freedom in America* (New York: Harcourt Brace Jovanovich, 1981), p.12; quoting from Elizabeth Donnan, *Documents Illustrative of the History of the Slave Trade in America* (New York: Octagon Books, 1965), Vol. 3, p.45.

26. Harding, op. cit.

27. Ibid.

28. Frederick Engels, *Origin of the Family, Private Property and the State*, p.231.

29. Engels, op. cit., p.319.

30. Ibid., p.247.

31. Ibid., p.232.

32. Diop, *Cultural Unity*, op. cit., p.19.

33. J.J. Bachofen was a historian who first researched the topic of the existence of matriarchy in the evolution of human society. In his book *Das Materrecht*, published in 1861, he argued that matriarchy existed everywhere at one time or another in all societies, before it was overthrown by patriarchy. Bachofen studied closely the traces of matriarchy found in the classical literature of antiquity, especially Greek and Roman. Morgan later (in 1871) confirmed Bachofen's views through research among native Americans of the Iroquois ethnic group resident in New York State. These he propagated in his work *Systems of Consanguinity and Affinity*.

34. Diop, *Cultural Unity*, op. cit., p.27.
35. Ibid., p.28.
36. Ibid., p.25.
37. Ibid., p.28.
38. Ibid., p.29.
39. Ibid., p.30.
40. Ibid., p.86.
41. Ibid., p.62. Here we are talking of Egypt before the Arabs occupied it comprehensively.
42. Ibid., p.36.
43. Ibid., p.68.
44. Ibid., p.69.
45. A.R. Radcliffe-Brown and D. Forde quoted in Diop, *Cultural Unity*, op. cit., p.71.
46. Diop, *Cultural Unity*, op. cit., p.125.
47. Hilda Kuper, *An African Aristocracy* (Oxford: Oxford University Press, 1969). I have grave reservations about studies such as these by anthropologists, missionaries and the like, which distort and misrepresent reality to suit their own racist notions about Africans. While this book falls squarely within this category, it does provide some useful information.
48. Kuper, op. cit., p.55.
49. Kuper, op. cit., p.91.
50. John Henrik Clarke's Introduction to Diop, *Cultural Unity*, op. cit., p.iv.
51. Diop, *Cultural Unity*, op. cit., p.116.
52. Williams, op. cit., p.113–15.
53. Diop, *African Origin*, op. cit., p.143.
54. Williams, op. cit., p.125.
55. J.H. Clarke in Introduction to Diop, *Cultural Unity*, op. cit., p.vi.
56. Ibid., p.vii.
57. Ibid., p.xi.
58. Williams, op. cit., p.276.
59. Ibid., p.284.
60. Ibid., pp.284–5.
61. Ibid., p.285.
62. J.D. Omer-Cooper, *The Zulu Aftermath* (London: Longman, 1966), p.87.
63. Ibid.
64. Ibid., p.88.
65. Tendai Mutunhu, "Nehanda of Zimbabwe: The Story of a Woman Liberation Leader and Fighter", in *Ufahamu* (filed in National Archives of Zimbabwe, Harare), p.60.
66. Ibid., p.63.

67. Tendai Mutunhu gives an excellent summary of Shona religious organization and why it played such an important role.

68. Terence O. Ranger, *Revolt in Southern Rhodesia 1867–70* (London: Heinemann, 1967), p.209.

69. Mutunhu, op. cit., p.65.

70. Ranger, op. cit., p.210.

71. Mutunhu, op. cit., p.68.

72. David Sweetman, *Women Leaders in African History* (London: Heinemann Educational Books, 1984), p.85.

The Role of Women's Organizations Within Southern Africa*

Olivia N. Muchena

The purpose of this paper is to examine the role of women's organizations as institutional vehicles for women's progress. These organizations can be seen as women's responses to their marginal position in society. In most of the Southern African Development Coordination Conference (SADCC) countries, women's organizations have been in existence for a long time. What changes or progress have these organizations brought to women's lives? Does the ideological orientation of a given country help or hinder the viability of women's organizations? What are the pros and cons of one all-embracing women's organization compared to many such groups co-existing within one country? Are separate women's institutions a positive or a negative factor in promoting women's integration in development? The necessarily limited responses given in this paper are aimed at stimulating further discussion for project ideas and/or policy formation.

There are three broad types of women's organizations within the regions under consideration. First, there are countries with a single all-embracing women's organization, usually the women's wing of the ruling party. The Organization of

*This paper was prepared for the conference "Women and Institutions in Southern Africa: Strategies for Change", hosted by the Ministry of Community Development and Women's Affairs in Zimbabwe, in Harare during November 1982.

Mozambican Women (OMM) and the Organization of Angolan Women (OMA) provide examples of this type.

Secondly, there are countries where in addition to the party's women's wing there are other women's organizations, most with international affiliations: for example, Women's Institutes (WIs), associations of country women's clubs, the Young Women's Christian Association (YWCA), to mention but a few. Membership of such organizations tends to be stratified, with the likes of WIs or women's clubs drawing their membership from the grassroots of urban and rural areas, while the YWCA and others tend to draw their membership from the rural or urban élite strata.

Within the second type is found a third type comprising women's organizations of indigenous origins, based either on traditional age-set groups or originating from within a community. Women's organizations of traditional origin do not appear to be as common in Southern Africa as they are in West Africa, for instance. Examples of community-originated organizations in Zimbabwe include the Association of Women's Clubs started by Helen Mangwenda, now a nation-wide movement.

With this typology in mind, let us attempt to answer some of the questions posed at the beginning of this paper.

A brief look at the track record of women's organizations can help us answer the question about the contribution that women's organizations can make to women's progress. In a 1979 study of women's organizations in Zimbabwe it was established that all of the groups interviewed (over thirty) had the general purpose of improving the quality of women's lives. They seek to do this through the following activities:

— home and health-care activities (cooking, nutrition, personal and family hygiene, etc.);
— social service/welfare activities (being of service to the needy within and without the organization, etc.);
— income-generating activities (sewing/dressmaking, keeping small animals, handicrafts, market gardening, etc.);

— educational activities (non-formal education, vocational and skills training, leadership training, pre-school education, etc.);
— agricultural activities (vegetable growing, water conservation, etc.);
— fund raising activities;
— civil and political activities (encouraging participation in community or local government bodies, courses of civic education, etc.).

Through such activities, women – not just in Zimbabwe but elsewhere in Southern Africa – have found channels for self-development and self-expression. It cannot be denied that women have made substantial achievements and contributions at personal, family, community and national levels. However, the question that must be answered is how significant have these changes been?

This leads us on to our next important question: what structural changes can women's organizations institute in a given society? Does the ideological orientation of a given country help or hinder the viability of women's organizations in effecting meaningful changes in women's lives?

Those women's organizations operating within a progressive ideological framework of their governments have more chance of effecting meaningful change in women's lives than would be the case in a less progressive or completely reactionary system. Illustrating this, the Organization of Mozambican Women (OMM) was originally established to mobilize women, "to teach them Frelimo's political line and to involve them in the revolutionary process".[1] The OMM has now been integrated into the planning groups at national and provincial levels, although both the party and the OMM are aware that women's participation at all levels must increase numerically.[2]

The advantage that the OMM would have over other women's organizations in a less favourable environment is that there is some constitutional basis for their government's commitment to changing women's position in society.

In what may be a unique constitutional provision Mozambique declares the emancipation of women as "one of the state's essential tasks".[3]

This type of statement and the revolutionary process leading to Mozambique's political independence is a much stronger basis for women's emancipation than is found in the usual general declaration of human rights, common in most constitutions whose primary concern was independence for the Africans of a given nation.

In the majority of SADCC countries, as things stand at the moment, women may not have the capacity and other prerequisites for effecting structural changes in their societies. In other words, they can only work within a given ideological framework with which they may or may not agree. How effective can women's organizations be in such situations in terms of making meaningful changes in women's lives? A simple answer is that they can certainly do better than at present. This, however, calls for a reassessment in conceptualizing and planning women's development programmes. A brief examination of the type of activities and approach to women's marginal position will illustrate the need for radical reorientation.

It is, sadly, true that for the past two or even three decades women have been perceived as needing nothing more than welfare improvement, as is evident from an examination of any of the women's programmes. Women's groups in Southern Africa have tended to prescribe a general welfare solution – through knitting, sewing, hygiene, nutrition and lately "income-generating" activities (whatever that means) – to problems that need economic, social or political solutions. How can you be all things to all women and hope to be effective? There has not been an adequate analysis of the situation of women in post-independence SADCC countries to determine whether mere improvement or radical transformation is called for. A clear perception of issues involved in each case is a prerequisite of effective programmes.

Another possible reason as to why women's activities have not made an impact, especially on the economic aspect of women's lives, is what I would like to call a project approach to development: the answer to women's problems is projects. But what are these projects?

Through the peripheral, piecemeal project approach women are supposed to generate income by means of handicrafts, poultry schemes, market gardening, tie-and-dye, etc. Let me illustrate what I mean by *peripheral* and *piecemeal*.

Women's projects are piecemeal in the sense that they are not part of the mainstream, not just of national development but even of the local district. Their projects are perceived in isolation from whatever else is going on. Take the poultry project, for example, in the middle of nowhere, or perhaps a weaving project. No feasibility study is undertaken to determine whether or not there is adequate infrastructure such as roads, or vehicles for transporting the eggs or products to the nearest market, which might be quite far away. Water might be a problem in the poultry project areas, so that women have to make additional trips to the well to fetch water for the chickens. In an effort to generate income, more burdens are given to the women, who are already overloaded. In other words, what relationship is there between women's projects and the local or national plans? Usually none, and so women continue in their piecemeal, isolated project approach as if they were a separate nation within the national development plans.

A second important aspect of the project approach that does not contribute to meaningful economic changes or gains for women is what I call the small-scale or income-generating mentality. Perhaps because women lack the education, financial resources and experience, women in development agencies at international level together with local women's groups have promoted the small-scale income-generating programmes. The drawback is that the projects are usually so small that virtually no income is generated after a great deal of effort, or if any income is generated it is not sustained for very long.

More significant is the tendency to think of women's enterprises in terms of "small". A women's group asking for $100,000 (Zimbabwean) for a vegetable-canning factory has no chance of getting any funding compared to those one thousand projects which are expected to be self-reliant within three years. Small may be beautiful but it can also be powerless and frustrating, besides perpetuating marginality. Women's organization leaders and their donors are both guilty here.

It appears that rather than sitting down, studying and analysing our own situations, determining our own priorities, we find it easier to react or respond to the prevailing or passing band-wagons. For instance, someone having discovered income generation a few years ago, income generation is now the in thing (even though tie-dye and clean water might be the priorities). Why don't we deal with things according to our own agenda and stick to it instead of imitating others, usually without doing any preliminary feasibility studies? If wealthy companies take time to do feasibility studies and decide on priority production targets why should women feel exempted?

It has been suggested in some quarters that the existence of numerous women's groups in one country, such as Zimbabwe, is a divisive factor in the women's struggle. This issue must be addressed seriously in order to determine its merits and demerits.

Does a single all-women's organization serve the interests of all women in a country or just the élite in leadership at whatever level? Are there enough checks and balances within such an institution to make it serve everyone's interests? On the other hand, the co-existence of numerous groups, usually formed on class lines, is not necessarily conducive to a united effort in a common cause. Most of these groups have international origins and affiliations. Does this not encourage dependency relationships when we are trying to work towards self-reliance?

Given the diversity of our historical and cultural experiences, it is up to each of our countries to work out what is the best possible strategy.

Whatever course is chosen should ultimately lead all countries with different women's organizations to answer the final question: does the existence of institutions to serve women's interests help or hinder women's progress? In order to address the age-old imbalances based on sex it is necessary to create special machinery for the advancement of women. However, if these institutions achieve their objectives, their existence need only be temporary because the situation will have been corrected and women will have an equal basis for competing equally with men for societal resources and benefits. A brief examination of current women's activities, however, would suggest that, for reasons such as ill-conceptualization of the problem and lack of holistic and long-term programme planning, it will be a considerable time before this happens.

Strategies for Change

The few ideas suggested below should serve to stimulate further thought, discussion and analysis in the hope that the emancipation of women will be promoted. They are not intended as answers or the final word but just one more step in the struggle for human rights in which women are involved.

1. Proper Definition of Problems

The late President Samora Machel of Mozambique said: "The fact that they [women] are exploited explains why they are not involved in all planning and decision-making tasks in society, why they are excluded in working out the concepts which govern economic, social, cultural and political life, even when their interests are directly related."[4] I want to suggest, as a first step, that women in Southern Africa study the concepts which govern economic and political life in their countries so that we understand what it is we are dealing with. When we talk about women wanting equal opportunities we are talking about power, economic and political, and yet we do not seem to understand or know how to get it and use it. Study the economic and political power structures. How do they operate? Where are the pressure points? How can these be used? How do we influence decisions? Proper conceptualization is a prerequisite of planning, while action not based on theory is mere activism.

2. Programme Planning

Let us abandon the piecemeal project approach and apply a holistic long-term coordinated perspective to planning. Governments and the business world spend months and years working out their development and business strategies. They want to be sure that they have the resources, that the different parts of the plans are complementary and inter-related. If women's efforts are to make an impact, more time should be put into planning action, monitoring and evaluation. What the position of women in SADCC countries will be in ten years from now should be a constant question to be answered by women's institutions.

3. Women's Organizations as Pressure Groups

It could be said that men generally perceive women to be potentially powerful, hence their often defensive attitude towards efforts to emancipate them. Women, on the other hand, do not seem to be aware of their potential for power. They bring up the children and have the power to influence the future generation's attitudes towards women. Women have a numerical strength in most SADCC countries, particularly in rural areas where as a result of male migration there are more women than men. And yet it is the same women who will vote for all-male local development bodies or councils.

There is a need for educating women to act as pressure

groups, to realize the power of their vote and the way it can be used to bargain for equal opportunities, credit facilities and social services, among other things.

Notes

1. Stephen and Barbara Isaacmen, *Mozambique: Women, the Law and Agrarian Reform* (1980), p.16. Frelimo, the Front for the Liberation of Mozambique (*Frente de Libertaçao de Moçambique*), was the Mozambican guerrilla movement that fought the Portuguese colonial regime.
2. Ibid., p.35.
3. Ibid., p.18.
Olivia N. Muchena, *Women's Organizations in Zimbabwe: An Assessment of their Needs, Achievement and Potential* (Harare: Centre for Applied Social Sciences, University of Zimbabwe, 1980).

II: Azania
(South Africa)

Introduction

Azania is an African country with a history as ancient as that
of countries such as Egypt and Ghana. Her vast mineral
wealth, moderate climate, arable lands and water resources
ensured the development of prosperous and advanced
civilizations; Africans here were skilled in the mining of
gold, iron and copper. Archaeologists have found evidence
of these civilizations at Palaborwa in today's Transvaal and
at Mapungubwe. Early European travellers observed towns
built with stone by Africans in the provinces of present-day
South Africa.

In the sixteenth and seventeenth centuries, several European
companies were involved in trade with Asia. En route to Asia,
they needed to trade in livestock, vegetables and fruit, and this
accounted for their initial presence on Azanian soil; once
there, the wealth of the country and its people encouraged the
Europeans to extend their stay. One such company was the
Dutch East India Company. On a journey in 1645 one of the
company's ships, the *Haarlem*, was wrecked at sea at Table
Mountain. The Dutch survivors came ashore and started
growing vegetables. On their return to Holland, their recommendations made the company decide to have a permanent
fort built in Cape Town, which would be a refreshment
station. Jan Van Riebeeck, who was on the *Haarlem* at the time
of the shipwreck, was to be in charge of this project. He was
told to remain if possible on good terms with the Africans,
mainly the Qhoi Qhoi (to whom the derogatory European
term "Hottentots" is applied), so that they could trade with
them for cattle. In the event that he should encounter any
difficulties with the indigenous people, they should be dealt

with firmly. Jan Van Riebeeck seemed able to implement the latter instruction more efficiently than the former.

From the outset he displayed an immense contempt for the indigenous people with whom he came into contact, the Qhoi Qhoi and the San, who had large herds of cattle as well as ivory and other items which the employees of the company needed. The Africans showed no hostility to the visitors and in fact were very friendly towards them. Trouble was started by Van Riebeeck and his crowd, who at first bought but later began to forcibly take cattle from the San. They also started stealing tracts of land.

This obviously did not please the indigenous people and numerous wars ensued. The Africans fought with outstanding courage but they could not match the superior weapons of the invaders. The survivors of these wars were massacred in cold blood by the Dutch colonists.

After their conquest of the Cape Peninsula, the Dutch proceeded to the interior but met fierce resistance. At no stage did the Africans accept settler confiscation of their land and livestock; they never stopped fighting. So successful were they in their wars of resistance that in 1836, nearly two centuries after the colonists first mounted their onslaught, Natal, the Transvaal and the Orange Free State provinces of today's South Africa were still under the control of the indigenous Africans. The most significant victories over the enemy forces were the Battle of Berea, where the British soldiers, who had now become rivals for control of the country's wealth, suffered a humiliating defeat at the hands of King Moshoeshoe's national army (near present-day Lesotho) and the Battle of Sandile's Kop where the Xhosa-speaking people wiped out three costly military villages of the enemies. One of the most brilliant victories scored was the Battle of Isandlwana in 1879, where 1,400 British soldiers were wiped out. Only 400 escaped. The last organized campaign of this nature was what later became known as the Bambata rebellion, which occurred in 1906, named after the leader who led and inspired it.

In 1795 the British colonists took control of the Cape. The British and the Dutch constantly argued among themselves about the best strategies to adopt in the colonization of the Africans. They also strongly vied with each other for physical control of the country.

By 1854 South Africa was already divided into distinct regions. The Transvaal and Orange Free State were controlled by the Dutch settlers and the Cape and Natal by the British settlers. British and Dutch rivalry increased with the discovery of diamonds and gold in 1867 and 1886 respectively in the Dutch-occupied areas of the Transvaal and Orange Free State, which led to wars between the two groups of colonists, notably the Anglo-Boer wars in 1871 and 1898. The settlers, however, always united against the Africans.

These wars ended in 1902, when the settlers signed the treaty of Vereeniging. (The treaty was followed by a referendum among the colonists – the British, Dutch, German and French.) In October 1908 a national convention was held in Durban to discuss the formation of the Union of South Africa. In pursuance of this, Britain passed the Act of Union (i.e. the South African Act) and sealed the fate of the indigenous Africans, who were at no stage consulted and whose interests were not taken into account. The Act was a result of a settlement between the two groups of colonists, both equally foreign to Azania. In May 1910, the "independent" Union of South Africa came into being. It introduced various statutes which consolidated colonial rule over Africans, the most notorious being the Land Act of 1913, which legitimized the theft of the last bits of fertile soil owned and controlled by black people.

It has been necessary to deal with the origins and process of colonization in Azania, for therein lies the root cause of the conflict now in the world headlines daily, namely the stealing of land from the Africans, who consequently suffered impoverishment, loss of life and human dignity and lack of advancement.

Two antagonistic forces whose interests are diametrically

opposed to one another are the main actors in this conflict. On the one hand there is the foreign settler-colonial nation comprising Europeans, predominantly of Dutch, French, British and German extraction, and on the other hand the dispossessed and colonized nation comprising the indigenous Africans and the black people of Asian extraction, brought to South Africa by the Dutch as indentured labourers. The nature of the 300-year-old conflict has not been altered by the passage of time. It will only be resolved on a permanent basis once the land is restored to its rightful owners, the indigenous African people.

The Position of African Women

European colonization of Azania had a dramatic impact on the lives of African women. From being respected members of society with a defined and valued economic, social and political role, they were reduced to landless farm labourers, domestic servants and perpetual minors.

The South African settler colonial state has, from the time that the first Dutch settlers set foot on Azanian soil until the present day, both covertly and overtly instigated and maintained measures geared toward the oppression and degradation of African women, while at the same time protecting and alleviating the lot of European settler women. From the outset Van Riebeeck and his fellow settlers, consisting of the crudest elements of Dutch society, took numerous liberties with the indigenous QhoiSan women, forcing them to become their slaves and concubines. This is how syphilis and gonorrhoea were introduced to this part of the continent.

In addition to venereal diseases, the European settlers also brought Christianity and a legal system derived in part from ancient Rome. It is this Roman-Dutch legal system which was to bode ill for African women. It entrenched, legitimized and enforced the socio-political measures introduced. What the colonists referred to as "customary law"[2] was "codified" to supplement this process of subordination. Because of their crucial role in the oppression of black women, it seems useful to look briefly at these laws in more detail.

Roman-Dutch law was the legal system of the colonists' mother country, Holland. A mixture of ancient Roman law and the common law of Holland at the time of the occupation of Azania, this is the legal system still used by the settler-colonial state. The unbelievably backward notions about women which the ancient Romans had were reflected in their laws. Women were regarded as feeble-minded, in need of constant supervision and protection from father, brother and husband. Women could not enter into contracts in their own right, nor could they acquire or dispose of property. They could do these things only with the "assistance" of their husband. (This refers to his consent, and in modern times to the actual appending of his signature to a document.) In Holland, as in other European countries, the situation was no different. Women could not hold public office and they were not allowed to obtain professional qualifications in order to practise a profession.

The Roman-Dutch law provisions relating to women remain unchanged, save for a few legislative amendments designed to ameliorate the effects of the common law on settler women's rights and legal capacity. In direct contrast, however, legislation has been introduced to ensure that African women are bound by the worst aspects of Roman-Dutch common law and what is termed customary law by the settler-colonial state.

Marriage in Roman-Dutch law has two sets of legal consequences, the invariable and the variable. The invariable consequences automatically ensure, without exception, that the husband becomes head of the household and guardian of his wife's person and has a duty to support his wife and children, etc. This law cannot be changed by parties before or during the marriage. The variable consequences are determined by whether a couple is married in community or out of community of property. At common law, all marriages are automatically in community of property. Parties in the marriage can, however, alter this by executing a document called an ante-nuptial contract prior to the marriage. The marriage is then out of community of property.

Where a marriage is in community of property, all assets owned by the husband or wife become the common or joint property of the couple in equal half-shares. Debts and other liabilities of each party whether incurred before or after the marriage also became the joint liability of the couple. In the event of divorce each spouse will be awarded one half-share of the assets of the marriage. This is perhaps the only positive aspect of this regime of marriage.

Most important in this type of marriage is what is termed the marital power of the husband, for it gives a man vast powers over the person and property of his wife. Only he has full legal capacity to act, even though he may be under twenty-one years old and the wife over twenty-one. It is from this power that the legal incapacity of the wife arises. By virtue of it, she cannot enter into any contract which binds her or her husband, without his consent. She cannot buy, sell or mortgage the common property on her own, even when it is in her name. She cannot stand surety in her own right.

She is, further, not able to institute legal proceedings other than for a divorce from her husband. She is said to have no *locus standi* – the right to be heard in court or other proceeding – and cannot be sued without her husband's authorization. In contract, the husband is the one to be sued. In torts or delict the action should be in the name of the husband in his capacity as her guardian. If a woman trades publicly, she may sign contracts but only those relating to her business.

In a marriage made with an ante-nuptial contract, all the variable consequences of a common-law marriage are usually excluded. The woman, therefore, retains full legal capacity. For example, she keeps her own property and deals with it as she pleases.

The settler woman, then, is able to choose her marital regime. Furthermore, legislation has been implemented to alleviate her common-law position. The most significant are the Matrimonial Affairs Act of 1953 and the New Matrimonial Property Act of 1984. The latter represents a major advance for European women for two reasons:

1. It enables parties to a marriage to abolish the husband's marital power within two years of the commencement of the Act and instead institutes a system of joint management where each spouse would be able to deal equally with the joint property. All they need do is to execute a notarial deed to this effect.

2. In the case of a marriage out of community of property, the accrual system will apply. This provides for the equitable distribution of property on the dissolution of the marriage in that it recognizes the contribution of both parties.

The South African state has decreed by legislation[3] that the African woman shall be considered in law a minor, no matter what her age actually is. She can be subject to either Roman-Dutch common law or what is purported to be customary law. However, it is not the woman who makes the choice but the commissioner of the courts set up by this legislation or the European legislator.

Section 27 of the Natal Code summarizes the attitude of the South African state to African women, and reads as follows:

Subject to Section 28 a female is deemed a perpetual minor in law and has no independent powers save as her own person and as specially provided in this code.

Section 28 provides that an unmarried female, a widow or a divorced woman who has money, property and is of "good character", educated and with "thrifty habits" can apply to the Commissioner's Court to be emancipated.

Further deliberate legal restrictions placed on African women include the express exclusion of African women from the provisions of the Matrimonial Property Act of 1984 discussed earlier; the provisions of Section 22 of the Black Administration Act which makes a marriage between Africans automatically out of community of property, while retaining the marital power. Unlike European women, therefore, African women cannot choose the regime according to which they wish to be married. They inherit the worst aspects of both regimes; whereas European women attain adult status on reaching the age of twenty-one or on marrying with ante-nuptial contract, African women never do.

All the above results in an absurd and very painful situation for indigenous African women, for regardless of their economic means, education or the fact that a large proportion of families are for all practical purposes female-headed due to the "migrant" labour system and other colonial practices, they are prevented from transacting even the most elementary business without the consent of a husband or male relative.

In other areas, African women occupy the lowest paid jobs. Even in the localities, where Africans are now allowed to buy land on a 99-year leasehold basis, women are not eligible for loans from building societies.

The violation of African women sexually and their alienation culturally are important mechanisms in the total subordination of the colonized African nation. On the one hand, sexual abuse of African women by European settler men is treated very leniently by both the police and the courts. These cases are rarely followed up by the police; where they are, the courts usually hand out very moderate fines or sentences, if the white defendant is found guilty. On the other hand, African men who rape white settler women are invariably sentenced to death or, in a few exceptional cases, given other heavy sentences.

Thus, a signal is sent out to the settler community in general, and settler men in particular, that African women are fair game. To African people, especially men, the message is that while their women can be defiled, settler women are sacrosanct and as such must not in any circumstance be tampered with by African men. This state of affairs is reminiscent of the period of legalized slavery in America, particularly in the southern USA, where African men would be lynched, hanged and castrated on occasion for doing no more than looking at a white woman.

The techniques adopted to effect and perfect the psychological oppression of African people in Azania are varied and sophisticated, largely due to the high level of industrialization and consumerism. It has been more successful than anywhere else on the continent. The attack is two-pronged.

First, the Azanian is denied the benefit of knowledge of the history and achievements, ancient and modern, of Africans, through an almost total ban on travel to other parts of the continent and a prohibition on literature which would serve as a source of information about such things. Secondly, anything and everything that is African is denigrated and conversely anything and everything that is European is deified, ascribing to white people all that is pure, advanced and beautiful. These racist myths are internalized. They engender feelings of inferiority and self-hatred and are destructive.

Black women, like women everywhere else who have been socialized into consumerism, are particularly susceptible to this type of anti-African propaganda. The European female image and European standards of beauty are aggressively flung at them daily, hourly, by the racist white-owned South African media. Typically African features such as full lips, naturally curly hair and dark complexions are presented as ugly. In pursuance of the white ideal, African women bleach their skins, straighten their hair and paint their faces; the result is a somewhat pathetic "carbon copy" of a European female. The skin-lightening creams applied to the face often cause disfigurement, sometimes permanently; mercuric oxide contained in these preparations is deposited in the kidneys and can cause renal damage. The hair straighteners, including the "perm curl" variety, break the hair and burn the scalp. The advertisers have apparently convinced these black women that their natural hair is "unmanageable" and "tense" and should be "relaxed" and made "manageable", irrespective of the financial and health hazards; in the process, the stunning beauty of African braids is in danger of being lost to all but a few conscious women.

The Black Consciousness Movement, of which Steve Biko

was one of the founding fathers and main ideologues, was the only black organization in the late Sixties and Seventies which addressed itself to this manifestation of colonial and racist oppression. After the banning of the various organizations under its banner, some of the new Black Consciousness organizations of the Seventies and Eighties appear not as concerned with these problems of mental colonization and cultural imperialism, though they have increased tenfold with the introduction of television and the intensification of the strategy which could be termed the "Americanization" of the African in Azania.

It is necessary to reiterate the fact that Azanian women were active and prominent members of their societies. Some of the more well known women were heads of state or regents. These included Queen Nonesi, the grandmother of a Paramount Chief, Sabata Dalinyebo of Tembuland; and Chieftainess Suthu, grandmother of Prince Maxhoba Yakhawuleza Sandile of Rarabeland. They executed their tasks as rulers efficiently. Later in Azanian history we have such women as Mma Ntatise of the BaTlokwa (see pages 53–5). King Shaka of the Zulus had an all women's regiment which very ably defended their land against the colonists.

Today, African women are trade unionists, underground organizers and couriers, trained guerrillas, wives of contract workers, supportive mothers, sisters and wives of freedom fighters. These countless women, whose names will probably never hit the headlines and who will probably never receive individual accolades, are nevertheless the cornerstones of the national independence struggle. To mention a few: Urbaniah Mothopeng, courageous wife and comrade of Zephania Mothopeng, the veteran African nationalist who at the age of seventy-three is spending his third term in a South African jail; Annie Silinga, who pledged in 1956 never to accept, or apply for, a permit-pass book and who, up to the day of her death on 30 June 1984, never carried one; Boniswa Ngcukana, militant of the PAC and brilliant trade-union organizer, murdered at Qasha's Nek on the Lesotho/South African border with five of her male comrades in March 1985; Theresa Ramashomola, sentenced to death along with five men in 1985 for her role in the uprisings which erupted in September 1984 in Sharpeville and other parts of the country – all six have appealed; Zodwa Sobukwe, wife of the late founding president of the PAC, Mangaliso Sobukwe, who because of victimization by the state has among other things never been able to practise her profession of nursing. Without their varied contributions, past and present, the struggle cannot be executed to its logical conclusion.

NOTES

1. My account of the history of European conquest relies on *The Story of a Dispossessed People* by Motsoko Pheko (London: Marram Books, 1984) and an unpublished paper by F. Njobe, *The National Question in Azania.*
2. The settler-colonial regime took certain aspects of African law and lifestyles, distorted them to suit its own purpose and presented them as customary laws. Thus, the regime conferred on African men the right to control the person and property of their wives, daughters and sisters and therefore eased the regime's job of keeping African women firmly in their place.
3. The Black Administration Act No.38 of 1927 and the notorious Natal Code of Black Law, which specifically applies to African women in the Natal Province.

The Right to Self-Determination
in Research: Azania and Azanian Women

Dabi Nkululeko

Azanians are waging an anti-colonial struggle, among other
struggles, yet their history is written by those who have
colonized them. If they are to avoid basing their policies,
programmes, strategies and tactics on the interpretations of
others, they must write their own history. After tasting the
pain of having to depend on information about them produced
by others and having seen the distortions, Azanians in
general, and women in particular, are becoming more and
more aware that one of the major fronts in the war against
colonialism is the writing of our own history.

The problems emanating from the violation of a people's
right to self-determination in research cannot be meaningfully
understood if the factors responsible are theorized separately
from each other in a manner that ignores their interrelation-
ship. Thus, to assert the need for native Azanian women to
determine the nature of the research undertaken about them,
and to do the research themselves, involves initiating discussion on the importance of a policy of self-determination for
the nation as a whole being accepted.

Can an oppressed nation or segment of it, engaged in a
struggle for liberation from its oppressors, rely on knowledge
produced, researched and theorized by others, no matter how
progressive, who are members of the oppressor nation? The
same question put in another way is: can the right of a people
to self-determination in the production of knowledge be
overlooked and liberation attained for them through knowledge produced by others?

This question arises in the context of an ongoing debate within the liberation movement in Azania, and internationally because certain trends were observed which indicate that some "progressives" see themselves as liberators of all the oppressed of the world while, on the other hand, the oppressed consider themselves their own liberators. Internationalist socialist "progressives" continue to show reluctance to abdicate their self-assigned leadership role, especially on the ideological front, and often fail to recognize the potential inherent in oppressed and exploited peoples to liberate themselves and to write their own history.

These same "progressives", instead of making the means of conducting research and study available to the oppressed and, thereby, enabling them to provide the wanting theory themselves in their otherwise enthusiastic struggles against imperialism, prefer to do the research on their own or with only the partial participation of the oppressed. Being the most subordinate and socially disadvantaged, African women have suffered most.

Yet, despite whatever limitations they may have, the products of a particular history arguably have the greatest potential to produce historical knowledge which can serve them in liberating themselves. This knowledge cannot best be determined by alien researchers, who will always be laden with the trappings of their own history, values, culture and ideology, regardless of how progressive they may be. As with other cases, the subjects of historical knowledge have the most legitimate right to carry out research and to write about themselves.

Until the middle of the twentieth century, and following some successes scored by the anti-colonial national liberation movements which attained independence in some African countries, research was conducted by colonist scholarship. The myth that natives were intellectually incapable of mastering the necessary know-how was used to exclude them. Hand-in-hand with this myth perpetuated by the colonists who settled in Africa went another myth, that with a researcher who was native to the subject country the element of bias would be so great as to render the findings less credible compared to those of an alien counterpart. It was assumed that the non-native, conversely, could separate herself from her own ideology and culture, her historical experience and from that of her subjects of study in order to produce value-free knowledge for "all", the colonizer and the colonized.

After independence in many African countries in the Fifties, Sixties and Seventies, doors opened to indigenous researchers and their biases were no longer thought to be any worse than those of their foreign counterparts. Racist attitudes were also checked by the surging African peoples' nationalism. However, still economically dependent on their ex-colonizers, African researchers found themselves largely at the mercy of their erstwhile masters. In order to win support for their selected topics of study they had to make sure that the funding agencies approved of the subject-matter. Obviously, donors approved topics that would most benefit them directly or indirectly. These donors were the leading and powerful governments and multinational corporations dominant in the global economic system; and this meant that the newly won right to self-determination was limited by economic dependence.

This complex new-yet-old relationship was called neo-colonialism: colonialism had simply assumed a new form, rather than having been eliminated as many thought. Women in the "neo-colonies" suffered most in terms of being able to study their own problems, since both the colonial and traditional legacies favoured education of men rather than women.

In our situation in Azania, what is claimed by some to have been independence (decolonization) in 1910, when the union of the four colonial states which now comprise South Africa took place, was worse than the neo-colonialism referred to above. The African and Asian people, who constituted four-fifths of the society, were further dispossessed and stripped of whatever meagre democratic rights they had before 1910. The minority settler-colonialists were given a blank cheque by their mother country to rule their colonial subjects directly and as they pleased.

Racist structures of oppression and exploitation were consolidated on to similar existing structures in order to guarantee the success of imperialism, which was now Anglo-American industrial and finance capital, having defeated German-Dutch settlers. In the case of Azania, therefore, instead of decolonization, a dominion of a colonial type was created and racism became a secondary manifestation of colonial national oppression. This level of perfected imperialist conquest was equalled half a century later by one other, that of the conquest, dispossession, oppression and exploitation of the Palestinian people by Israeli settler-colonialism. The native women of Palestine and Azania were subordinated to settler-colonialism, racism (Zionism and apartheid) over and above class and sex subordination.

Factors Restricting Indigenous Research

The native researcher's position of subordination to knowledge determined by alien researchers became intolerable. Research was confined to those topics or questions which the colonialist and racist power structure was willing to tolerate. Even when out in exile, those who fled from the settler and mandated colonies faced neo-colonial constraints: dependence on the ex-colonial masters of these countries, or their allies.

The constraints on the native researcher were not only those mentioned above. Her task was made more difficult, if not impossible, by her dependence on theoretical tools and constructs developed by theorists from other parts of the world, areas of their own concern. It is incumbent upon the native researcher to critically analyse these and, if they are appropriate, to develop them. But more important, she must overcome her dependence on them and develop new theories, constructs and concepts which, above all, capture what is real in Africa. This will enable her to problematize and suggest methods of making revolution. Only then can she liberate

91

herself from theoretical tools of research which were intended for other situations or for perpetuating colonial and racial domination. She can then respond, unrestricted, to the demands for knowledge produced for the needs of her emergent society.

Sympathizers with the revolution in Africa can only play a supportive role (not determinant) in this struggle for self-determination. In a broad sense, the same applies to sympathizers with the emancipation of women from sexism. On the question of the liberation of women, women themselves within the nation must produce knowledge required for their own emancipation and do so through research which takes their experience into account.

It must not be overlooked, however, that the native researcher, like her alien counterpart, has to overcome her class stand in order to take a class position opposing, as the oppressed have done, imperialism. Because she is of petty-bourgeois origin and has inherited the ideological trappings of her class, she too could take a class position which favours imperialism and not the oppressed and exploited masses. Over and above this, she has been alienated to a certain extent from her cultural heritage and, therefore, its tools of conceptualization. Hence, she must consciously employ her cultural heritage and tools of conceptualization. This means going beyond the present boundaries of theorization, beyond scholasticism, to the addition of new facts and/or the challenge to old ones.

The non-native who wants to study people outside his/her own culture and historical experience has an almost impossible task – that of trying to be what she is not in order to be an "Africanist" theoretician.

The theory of self-determination in research applies to any nation or segment thereof, not necessarily the colonized. If an African wanted to study the history of the German or the English, she would have to step out of her own situational culture into that of her subjects of study. This is an equally difficult task for the African researcher as well.

Azania as Case Study

Azania will serve as an example of problems, which are not unique to her but also common to other colonies, concerning the alien domination in research.

Initial Modern Intellectual Opposition

After the colonial forces had managed to subordinate the people of the country we now call Azania, in the last decade of the nineteenth century, a new movement was born to combat or to minimize colonial oppression. Racist structures which were introduced at the same period confused some in this civil-rights movement, causing them to focus more on its structure and attacking them for injustice. There were others within this movement who concerned themselves more with the issue of self-determination for the African people, and called upon all Africans to unite into one nation and demand their right to self-determination. These saw racism as part of the colonial strategy of conquest and subordination, and not a shift from colonialism.

Both the liberal and socialist "progressives" referred to above did not trust the latter group. They could not tell how far this struggle for self-determination would go and they feared for their own interests. They called the new nationalism among Africans "racism" and "separatism" because it rejected their tutelage.[1]

These "progressive" colonists put their resources where their own interests were by supporting the mild democratic and élitist African movement which demanded civil rights such as the right to the franchise, the right to buy land, the right to an education, etc. – in short, racial equality. This group was favoured because it no longer pursued the cause for the repossession of the lost motherland, nor opposed capitalism as a system of production that accelerated the rate of exploitation of African labour.

Radicalization within the Protest Movement

It was in this respect that the new nationalist movement failed to get support for its research programme (aimed at re-writing the history of the African people). Instead, support was showered on those who wanted to write about racial equality. Those who wanted to do research on the demand for the right of African peoples to national self-determination were excluded through financial starvation. Funds were made available only to those who were prepared to toe the line.

This meant that in Azania people from abroad, and from the ranks of the oppressor nation, who attacked the racist character of the state came to dominate research and be the ones to problematize and set the ideological pace. The national liberation movement was divided because not all gave into this line. The new tendency questioned the very dependability of the colonizers to produce knowledge for the liberation of the colonized.

I would like to mention also that the ideology of scientific socialism, as a guide to action and a tool of analysis, was subsequently distorted and vulgarized by its exponents, the so-called "progressives". When national struggle surfaced within it, it was deemed reactionary. At this point I will refer to a paper by Tony Mabona on "Liberation and its History in Azania", which discusses the link between liberalism and the self-proclaimed socialists of the British Labour Party.[2]

It is at this juncture that the national as opposed to the anti-discrimination movement became concerned about the right of the African to self-determination in the writing of the history of Azania.

It became clear that the non-native was unconscious not only of the demands of the native but also of the national identity of the natives; that his or her limited awareness resulted from the fact that it was an opposing force to them, a force with its own interests and identity. In the case of Azania this was revealed by the denial or trivialization of African nationalism and culture, and its rejection as a subjective force with a role to play in the revolution, by liberals, socialists ("progressives") and conservative colonists alike.

Having fully realized self-determination for themselves, settler scholarship, which was aware of and participated in struggles between the colonizer and the colonized, assumed that the Africans who were still waging the old struggles against the colonizer did not need to do so as a people (a nation) but as a race. This element could not be party to that, as it brought out, first and foremost, the contradiction between the researchers and their subjects of study, the natives. This is why the alien researchers, denying that the natives were still fighting for their land, for control of the products of their own labour, for self-determination, only supported the anti-colour-bar struggle which did not go deeper into the problem.

As the birth of national liberation movements in the presently independent African countries was inspired by the birth of African nationalism in Azania early this century, following the formation of the African National Congress (ANC), so in the 1940s were the youth in the ANC inspired, in turn, to revive the latent nationalism of the last and first decade of the nineteenth and twentieth centuries respectively, by the re-emergence of nationalism among their brothers elsewhere on the continent.

With the pace of decolonization accelerating in the 1950s, the demand for self-determination and the possible birth of independent African nations was no longer a vision, but a reality. If it could be realized in other parts of Africa, why not in their own part? The ideal of African national independence in South Africa still remains elusive, together with the ideal of taking over the responsibility to write our own history.

Further Contemporary Theories on Struggle

In spite of these developments, research continued to be dominated by alien/settler scholarship, as the late 1960s and 1970s saw "progressive individuals" who were prepared to go beyond the anti-apartheid stance to an anti-capitalist and anti-imperialist strategy, but still failed to recognize the leading and central role to be played by the indigenous oppressed people in their own liberation in every area of struggle, including academic and research.

The new theories have yet to be evaluated, but there is no harm in pointing out a few methodological problems: for example, the seemingly radical theories of underdevelopment and dependency advanced by Gunder Frank and others and the fact that the oppressed are credited with no initiative by the new school. Things are done to them, but they in turn are not keen to do things to those who oppress and exploit them. These theorists do not seem to see the struggle as being between two sides.

The anti-imperialist struggles waged by the people and their demands are ignored or labelled reactionary. This is how they are kept out of the history books. Johnstone sees the national question, colonial and ethnic, and questions other than race and class, as unnecessary layers mystifying history.[3] Legassick, on the other hand, concentrates on accumulation of capital through the exploitation of labour. To him, change in South Africa means: "Production must be maximized, distribution equalized and control centralized."[4] Legassick's kind of change does not take into consideration the national democratic revolution and its agrarian component as a necessary stage in the revolution for the emancipation of labour from capital. One is left wondering as to the motives behind this adamant denial.

This issue of a research priority list which responds to the demands of the masses becomes more urgent as one reviews the literature. The myth that natives are incapable of mastering research techniques and methods has been blown by the few, but qualitatively significant, works produced by the rejected native scholars who refused to limit themselves to the ceiling skilfully placed by their colonist counterparts. Participatory observation and participatory research which were used to complement this myth were also discredited with it. Understandably, imperialist-funded sources are still, by and large, not prepared to support, let alone publish, the research and findings which can fuel the struggles of the oppressed nations and classes of the world to overthrow them. Until the national liberation movement itself comes to terms with the importance of research, this situation will continue.

What this means, essentially, is that the alien researchers continue to dominate research and as such remain the ideological leaders of the colonially oppressed and dependent nations, as was the case under classic colonialism. It also means that independent research organizations must look to themselves for funding and must rededicate themselves to the decolonization of research, and as such to the decolonization of our history.

The history of Azanian women has also been written by alien researchers. For the same reason discussed, African women either do not have the necessary educational background and/or the funds needed to do research and determine priority questions to be investigated.

The result of this is that the alien scholars, mainly female, still examine, report and analyse the role of the Azanian woman, focusing on whichever of the forms of oppression they saw as important for themselves and harping on that until the other forms were forgotten by all except those who suffered them.

The over-emphasis on apartheid, to the exclusion of colonialism, class exploitation and sex oppression, is an example of this practice. The anti-apartheid movement forced its own views and theories about the oppression of women in Azania in order to shift the emphasis away from the anti-colonial strategy, with repossession of the territory and the right of self-determination, to one of reformism which demands that racial equality and civil rights – the right of citizenship for the African and Asian peoples – can and ought to be granted to them by the alien state of South Africa.

The Primacy of the Land Question and the Anti-Colonial Struggle

The difference between the two strategies discussed above is vast. The anti-colonial strategy rejects colonial occupation and dispossession of the native people by aliens, while that employed by progressives such as the anti-apartheid movement condones it and accepts it as a *fait accompli* and sees civic reforms as the only solution. The anti-apartheid movement, therefore, sees the oppression of women as the result of the deprivation of civil rights to African women, while the anti-colonial movement sees it as a consequence of the colonial expropriation of their livelihood and land, forcing them to sell their labour and bodies to their dispossessors, the settler-colonial capitalists. The scheme of things deprived women of their fundamental right to make and write their own history, and is the link between the various forms of oppression experienced by women, namely colonialism, racism, class and sexism.

The use of the means of production as a basis for exploitation and oppression of African women, as a segment of the colonized nation, is essential to their remaining the racially discriminated against, the exploited labour force and finally the sexually discriminated against victims of imperialism. It is also the cord with which Azanian women link their struggle to the demands of the nation.

The oppression of women is therefore four-fold. All four types of oppression are forms of the manifestation of imperialism in our country and must be seen in their order of priority to guarantee that the women's struggle for emancipation does not counter but rather reinforces the entire anti-imperialist struggle.

The struggle and suffering experienced by women in Azania can, therefore, be equated with that of women throughout the Third World. The violation of their right to self-determination in research is common, in one way or another, to all of them. Despite the limited participation by women of the Third World in the research undertaken about them, Third World women produce qualitatively more material on their own oppression than their counterparts. Women of Western Europe, for example, understand sexism in their class societies but fail to understand it in the more complex situation of the Third World, where class and sex oppression are joined by colonial and racial oppression.

Stephanie Urdang saw two forms of oppression against women in Guinea Bissau[5] – what she calls two colonialisms or a dual oppression, meaning Portuguese colonial oppression and male oppression. What about class oppression and racial oppression, which were also practised by the Portuguese and their Guinean lackeys?

On the other hand, the writers on women in Azania tend to blot out white women and their own oppression, and to reduce oppression of African women to race and sex domination. Again here the view of dual (as opposed to quadruple) oppression is favoured. Kimble et al.[6] see race, class and sex oppression yet ignore colonialism, which is the primary manifestation of imperialism in Azania. They see South Africa, born out of an Anglo-Boer compromise and exclusion of the African and Asian peoples, as one nation consisting of "Blacks" and "Whites". To them, national liberation means Blacks and Whites integrated and fighting for a democratic society without race, class and sex oppression. The fact that Africans and Asians – particularly women – in that country do not enjoy the right to determine their own fate and make as well as write their own history does not seem to be their concern, despite the fact that it is the very loss of this right which determined the racial and class position of the said peoples and placed African women on the lowest rung of that society.

Colonialism was the gateway for imperialism. Only after the African people were conquered, and dispossessed of their wealth and their stock, was it then possible for the colonist settlers to occupy the territory and to oppress the indigenous people racially and to exploit and abuse African women. Only then were the landed aristocrats and the capitalists able to oppress the Africans and Asians racially, classwise and sexwise. Before the colonial occupation of Azania by the merchant companies and their colonists, the women experienced class and sexual subordination to some degree – like other women whose countries have passed from primitive communalism to feudalism, but are not colonized.

The advent of colonialism further weakened the position of women in relation to the means of production, putting them in a position where they had to work the land for the alien settlers, as opposed to working the land for themselves, their husbands and their children. In this new position, women were deprived of their source of livelihood. They became wives of squatters, slave labourers, and later wives of wage-earners. None of these incomes met the needs of the women and their children. So the women themselves became slave labourers and later wage workers for the colonists, who were both male and female.

Black and White Women: the Effects of Sexism and Colonialism

The role of the colonist-settler women in the oppression of the native women is yet to be investigated, but as a segment of the colonizing people (nation) they played a major role in and are direct beneficiaries of colonial and racial oppression of the native people (nation), including native women.

Without the solution to these problems one is only being illusory and extremely hypothetical in opposing racism and imperialism on one hand and, on the other, ignoring or denying its very roots. This denial is responsible for the further denial or neglect of the role settler women have played in perpetuating sexism against native women (their domestic servants) and for the pretence that natives are part of the settler nation of South Africa. It is also responsible for the neglect of the fact that women in Azania do not constitute one segment of society but two segments, which are not oppressed in the same way.

Settler women occupy a class, position and status which is above that of their native counterparts, male and female. For example, Euro-settler women researchers enjoy privileges which their male and female subjects who are native do not enjoy. They have liberal access to financial, educational and social facilities. This is the reason why settler women manage to write about the natives, not because they are more intelligent or more willing.

Native women cannot take up such a task until they are supported by the liberation movement and its allies and provided with the necessary resources. As long as this does not happen on a large scale, the oppression of native women will remain only partly explained because it is the native women themselves, as the oppressed, who can best explain and help others to understand it.

As aliens to this experience, Euro-settler women have to overcome most of the trappings of their own experience (historicism), such as their own class interests and status, and they have to first study closely their experience as part of the colonist-settler nation, dissociate themselves from it before they can begin to comprehend the experience of the native women under colonialism.

It is not enough to denounce racism, to join the ranks of the African national liberation movement and turn one's back on one's own sisters, mothers and daughters (who unleash oppression on the native women) because it is they who need to be shown the wrong in so doing. *In order to extricate themselves from culpability in the oppression of African women, settler women – the "feminist socialists" must work among their own people to create conditions for the destruction of such oppression, while their counterparts among the native women must do the same within their own ranks.*

The work which both must do to create such conditions will have to include theorization of the social relations between the two segments and their respective nations, the nature of the struggle which goes on and the connection between that struggle and other struggles in the society as a whole. It will have to locate women in the order of priority in the society as a whole.

The claim that African women have not spelled out their demands, and that women's oppression has been seen as stemming from and explained in terms of the colour bar,[7] is attributable to the myopic and sectarian approach of those writers who limit themselves only to the anti-apartheid and intergrationist trend of the liberation movement, excluding the other trends because they do not favour them.

The ambiguous concept of African nationalism referred to as "the building of a self-confident and strong African nation in South Africa" is contradicted by the call for a United Democratic Front, as opposed to a demand for the right of the oppressed nation (African) to self-determination. Such a call has contributed to the failure to understand women's oppression in that country on the part of the Western feminist.

The present African nation is confused with the envisaged nation-to-be, in which both settlers and Africans will have united, after decolonization has taken place and national oppression of the Africans by the settlers has ended. The result of this confusion is the integration policies which have led to Euro-settler trusteeship over the native peoples' programmes for national liberation, something which consistently divides the national liberation movement into violently opposed groups, for and against Euro-trusteeship. Nationalists ask: where is the self-determination, if we are yet to be patronized by "progressive Whites"?

Self-determination in research, especially for women, is also washed down the drain by integrationism. Under the guise that those who prefer self-determination to colonist tutelage are separatist and racist, the "progressive Whites" – feminists included – go on every international forum with a big stick, clobbering any native researcher and writer who is independent from them in thinking, while nestling those who depend on them for ideological guidance and for leadership generally.

In this way, independent-thinking African nationalists have been denied expression, making it difficult for them to theorize the links between national oppression, class exploitation, racial oppression and sexism, all of which constitute the manifestation of imperialism in our country. The integrationists want to cover up national oppression by artificially integrating the oppressor and the oppressed into a democratic alliance before national oppression has been eliminated. This misleading strategy, if not condemned and fought, will continue subverting the people's struggle for national liberation.

It is at this conjuncture that the theory of self-determination is advanced, and a call is made to the liberation movement to provide resources for the few independent-thinking native researchers to work as activists and theoreticians. The work by Kimble *et al.* previously referred to, is sectarian in its approach because it limits itself to women whose views run concurrently with the anti-apartheid line and excludes those who see imperialism as fundamental and colonialism as its primary form. Denial of the primary role of colonialism is the epitome of the confusion about which nation is oppressing which, and therefore, what the content of the national liberation struggle is and what the women's emancipation struggle should entail.

African Women, Literature and the National Liberation Movements

Under the four-fold barricade of imperialism, the few works by African women, such as one by Nomfundo Luswazi,[8] emerge as pace-setters for Azanian women who do not take their cue from the women of the West. Space does not permit a critique of all the works (for example, Kimble *et al.*); but suffice it to say that they fail to examine the various, but linked, forms of manifestation of capitalist exploitation (i.e. imperialism in our era) individually first, in order to understand the characteristics of each form, their interdependency and movement and where their links are weak, then to help the struggling masses and to devise effective strategies, programmes and tactics.

As women represent the most oppressed segment of society (more oppressed than even the oppressed men in each society) and constitute the majority, they are an essential part of the struggle of the oppressed in each society. For this reason they must resist attempts to subordinate them and undermine their role in the struggle against the other forms of oppression, and in the creation of a programme against sexism in their society.

In Azania, it is being suggested that women themselves have not problematized sex oppression; that women's oppression stems from apartheid; that they must, therefore, struggle for racial equality. The special disabilities of women are seen as constituting their triple oppression . . . *and it is primarily through the main struggle that women will gain their rightful place.*

This rightful place is left vague and obviously depends on what the male-dominated leadership of "the main struggle" deems it to be. Triple oppression here means race, class and sex oppression; it does not include national oppression. Women cannot afford to leave their fate in the hands of males, since the male-dominated system has provided men with a status which allows them to abuse women. Nomfundo Luswazi calls for an independent women's organization.

If women are not organized as women, and do not determine their own liberation but are only organized within the male-dominated sections of society or the liberation movement generally, as suggested above, what will prevent the male leadership from continuing the old relationship which guarantees them privileges over their women, at least? I say "at least" because African men are oppressed themselves and are not the ultimate beneficiaries of the oppression and exploitation of women. The principals of international finance capital are the main beneficiaries and their agents, the settler-colonists, are next in line. Luswazi comments on the need for self-determination for women, viz:

How can the Black women change their specific situation which capitalism has enforced on them? How can the black women fight against male chauvinism?

How can black revolutionary women contribute best towards national liberation and for a socialist Azania under the firm control of the proletariat, which is a prerequisite for the proletarian women to fully emancipate themselves at all levels in society? . . .

You can only mobilize people on the basis of their concrete problems, and those who are part of the solution must decide all questions concerning their problems.[9]

On behalf of the Isandlwana group, she pointed out:

Hence we believe that future Azanian women patriots and revolutionaries will, besides organizing themselves in different anti-colonial and anti-capitalist organizations of our people, also go ahead and organize black women's organizations.[10]

Without counterposing women against men as such (which would be divisive) women have to be provided with know-how and resources which will enable them to stand on their own feet. Emphasis is on the toiling women because these have not yet been brought into the organized movement for liberation as much as men have been. And this is because of the day-to-day problems confronting them, ranging from the basic necessity to survive with their children to problems with government bureaucrats and pass-permit raids.

In conclusion, women in Azania have made clear demands and have shown that they can respond to the most challenging tasks when organized and relieved of the compelling day-to-day (and yet never-ending) struggles for self and children, to the wider yet specified struggles for national and social liberation, of the colonized from the colonialists and labour from capital, etc.

Women cannot rely solely on those who are party to their oppression for the solution to the contradiction between the sexes. The programme for their transformation from the dependent, unskilled, weak-bodied and weak-minded creatures (with no access to private and/or social property) must be determined by them. Their own experience can be aided by their own efforts to do research and recommend a programme for their liberation based on their findings rather than on what others think.

NOTES

1. Kahn *et al.*, *From Protest to Challenge* (California: Sheridan Johns, 1972), p.8.
2. Tony Mabona, "Liberation and its History in Azania", special issue of *Isandlwana*; also Legassick, "South Africa, Capital Accumulation and Violence", in *Economy and Society*, Vol.3, No.3 (1974), pp.283–4.
3. Frederick Johnstone, "Most Painful to our Heart: South Africa Through the Eyes of the New School", in *Canadian Journal of African Studies*, Vol.16, No.1 (1982), pp.6–7.
4. Legassick, op. cit. Legassick sees colonial oppression as "internal Colonialism practised by the Whites". He, like most alien scholars, denies the character of the South African state and its electorate.
5. Stephanie Urdang, *Fighting Two Colonialisms: Women in Guinea-Bissau* (New York: Monthly Review Press, 1979).
6. Judy Kimble *et al.*, *We Opened the Road for You, You Must Go Forward, ANC Women's Struggles 1912– 1982*, p.14.
7. Ibid., p.28.
8. "The Women's Question in Azanian Revolution", in *Isandlwana* (official organ of Isandlwana Revolutionary Effort of Azania), No.8/9, July–Sept/Oct–Dec. 1981, pp.18–44.
9. Ibid.
10. Ibid.

Interview with Nomvo Booi*

A very special participant in the celebration of International Women's Day on 8 March 1983 was Mrs Nomvo Booi. She has belonged to the Pan-Africanist Congress of Azania (PAC) since the very beginning of the movement and was Regional Secretary in the Transkei, among other things; she is presently a member of the Central Committee of the PAC. The following glimpse of her political life, which has spanned more than thirty years, also illustrates how strongly the life of an Azanian woman is influenced by the choice to take part in the political struggle.

Nomvo, could you tell us something about your political activities – how you started and how things went on?

At a very young age I became a member of the African National Congress (ANC). I was involved in the successful "Defiance Campaign"[1] in 1952. What a great power of the masses we saw then. At that time I was a member of the ANC Youth League, which held the opinion that the ANC leadership stopped the campaign too quickly and too easily. This Youth League formed the foundation of the PAC, which was formed in 1959. I was closely involved in its founding. I was a district secretary of the PAC by then.

During the Positive Action Campaign of 1960, which ended in the Sharpeville massacres, a State of Emergency was

*This interview was conducted by a member of the Azania Committee, a Dutch organization working in solidarity with the struggle of the Azanian people, in London, March 1983.

declared. I lived in Queenstown in the Transkei then. I was arrested during the emergency. I went into prison for four months. After that event I went underground, working for POQO.[2] After my imprisonment I could not find a job in Queenstown, so I lost the right to live there. In 1961 I moved to the Transkei. There I continued working underground for POQO. In August 1962 I was arrested again for suspected PAC activities. I was put into prison for ninety days without trial, without my family knowing where I was, without extra clothes, without something to read. The ninety days were multiplied into two hundred and seventy days, and afterwards into eleven months. During this time I was constantly in isolation, was constantly interrogated.

When we asked her to talk about the torture she was subjected to, Nomvo swallowed and told us that she was not able to talk about the matter. It was clear to us that she had had a hard time. She said quickly:

Be it enough for you if I tell you that since then I am suffering from backaches, rheumatism and painful feet; but the political story is more important, so I will continue that one.

After eleven months there was a trial. During this trial I was convicted and sentenced to three years in jail by virtue of the Suppression of Communism Act. During this period BOSS[3] tried to buy me and asked me if I wanted to work for them. I refused. After these three years in prison I was banned to Willowvale, in a very remote area. From the end of 1968, when I was "freed", I was followed constantly by policemen and they constantly invaded my house. This situation continued until December 1982, when finally I was forced to go into exile. From 1968 till 1982 I lived in the Transkei and Ciskei. In November 1982 I was arrested without reason and kept in custody for a week. After this I fled into Lesotho. After my stay here in London I will probably go to Tanzania working for the PAC. Before I came to London I was in Vienna to represent the PAC at the International Women's Congress organized by the United Nations in support of the struggling women of Southern Africa.

Is your family still in Azania?

My eldest daughter (twenty-five years old) is in Azania. I don't know where she is and what is happening to her.

Stella Moabi, a member of PAC working in its West German office, was also present during this talk with Nomvo and asked her how many times she had been in prison. Nomvo replied that she is not the only one and that in fact all this does not matter so much. After some pressure from our side, here follows her sad list:

1. Queenstown
2. East London (where she was in solitary confinement and almost broke her neck)
3. Engcobo
4. Umtata
5. Moanduli (in solitary confinement)
6. Idutywa (in solitary confinement)
7. Again in Engcobo
8. Kroonstad
9. Pretoria Central Prison
10. Nylström
11. Again in Umtata.

Proudly, Nomvo tells us the following story about Pretoria Central Prison:

I was there together with other political prisoners in one cell. At breakfast we got porridge without a spoon and without sugar. All together we asked for spoons and sugar. Then we were taken out of the cell and accused of mutiny! The white guard refused to deal with rebellious prisoners like us. That's why we were taken to Nylström, where a part of the prison was specially organized for "heavy" prisoners, which we were supposed to be . . . .

Everything in your life is a struggle! Something else: all these years of prison, bannings and persecution by the police – what gave you the power to continue?

How could I stop? You just have to go on and on. My children have already suffered a great deal, my people are suffering. I never asked myself that question: whether or not to go on with the struggle. Sometimes it was difficult, however; when I was banned in 1966, I wished I was still in prison. There I was locked up but I had a little bit of food, soap, a roof over my head. In banishment I had nothing: no work, no house, no money.

How for God's sake did you survive?

I wrote letters to Vorster, who was at that time Minister for Justice, and finally I got the permission to go to another district, where a brother of mine helped me with a room and work. I got a job there working on a bus. And I sewed clothes for other people.

What happened to you after 1968?

After my banning I left the Transkei at the end of 1968. Churchpeople asked me to help women who were deported far away, dumped in the Ciskei. The church had organized three sewing-machines for women – this was a Roman Catholic church, led by white people, attended by black people. They did a good job. I went to to work among the women, and with success, until there came a crisis in Fort Hare University. The clergymen were banned because of so-called "subversive activities". The church could not support our group and we had to stop our activities. Then I continued my work amongst the women and built up another group. I taught them to sew, so that they could earn their own living. Of course all this had to be done in deepest secrecy. It cost a lot of sacrifices and I only got a very small amount of money for it.

It must have been very, very difficult to work with women under these conditions and to make them politically conscious. Did you find a way to do so?

Sure I did! Look, the position of these women was of course very difficult; they had to live there alone with their children, their husbands lived far away, working in the mines. They had to do everything themselves: working in the fields, household work, educating the children. They were not able to earn their living by a profession. To teach them how to sew, in fact, was working for the first political purpose of the PAC: to help people help themselves! Of course I did not talk about the fact that I am a PAC member. When you are working underground, it is difficult to know who you can trust and who you cannot trust.

NOTES

1. A campaign of civil disobedience.
2. The armed wing of the PAC, now called the Azanian People's Liberation Army (APLA).
3. The Bureau for State Security, the South African intelligence organization.

Lilian Masediba Ngoyi
(1911–80)

Lilian Masediba Ngoyi – affectionately known as "Ma-Ngoyi" – was one of the best known and most highly regarded anti-government campaigners in Azania. Born in Pretoria on 25 September 1911, she spent her first years of activism as a member of the Garment Workers Union (GWU); in 1952 she and her daughter were among the thousands who marched in protest against the banning of Solly Sachs, Secretary-General of the GWU.

Lilian was an effective organizer and a brilliant orator, and this, combined with her strength of character and dedication to her beliefs, saw her become a member of the National Executive Committee of the African National Congress (ANC) and, in 1956, President of the Women's League and the Federation of South African Women. In 1954 she went on an international tour which took her to China, the German Democratic Republic and to other countries in Europe.

In 1955 it was announced by the then Minister of Native Affairs that African women would have to carry passbooks for the first time, effective from January 1956. This arbitrary extension to women of the oppressive pass laws provoked nationwide demonstrations. Numerous protest marches were organized. The first took place in October 1955 with 2,000 women; however, the best known one was led by Lilian Ngoyi a year later, when 20,000 women from various parts of the country assembled in Pretoria to deliver a petition to the office of Prime Minister J.G. Strijdom, on 9 August – a day since designated as "Women's Day".

Lilian's political activities resulted in her being constantly harassed by the South African regime. She was arrested in 1956, together with the 155 other defendants in the notorious four-year Treason Trial, and placed in solitary confinement for nineteen days.

In 1960, the Pan-Africanist Congress of Azania (PAC) organized a nationwide anti-pass campaign. The South African regime reacted with violence, shooting dead and injuring scores of people in Sharpeville in the Transvaal and in Langa in Cape Town. A State of Emergency was declared when the regime could not control the uprising through violence and the banning of the ANC and the PAC followed. During this period Lilian was detained for five months.

In 1961, she was served with a five-year banning order which prevented her from being quoted or attending any meetings; from October of the following year she was restricted to her house in Orlando, Soweto, and so was forced to give up her job and to rely on sewing at home, though the Special Branch scared her customers away. Not until November 1972 was this banning order lifted.

Lilian's spirit was not broken during these years of restrictions, however, and she immediately resumed her public commitments and political activities in 1972. She actively encouraged young people to fight the South African government; "If I die, I'll die a happy person because I have seen the rays of our new South Africa rising," she was quoted as saying in January 1980 (in *Sechaba*). Her outspokenness and campaigning led in 1975 to a further banning order for another five years. On 12 March 1980, less than two months before the expiration of this banning order, Lilian Ngoyi died from natural causes.

Her death was a great loss to the ANC and to black people as a whole. Thousands of mourners attended her funeral on Heroes' Day, 21 March 1980, honouring her as a symbol of resistance and inspiration. In 1983, as the highlight of a series of events held to commemorate the twenty-seventh anniversary of the historic 1956 march, the Federation of South

African Women organized the unveiling at Lilian Ngoyi's grave of a tombstone in tribute to her contribution to the anti-government struggle.

Exemplifying the necessity for women to participate as equals in the freedom movement, Ma-Ngoyi will surely be remembered when Azania gains its independence.

Interview with Sibongile Mkhabela (née Mthembu) *

Sibongile Mthembu came into political prominence during the June 1976 uprising in Soweto. She is probably one of the most intractable political prisoners the South African police state has had to deal with. She came to trial in 1978 at the age of twenty, after spending a little over two years in police custody. Despite severe torture, she was unbending in her resolve not to incriminate other student leaders and her unwillingness to regard herself as a criminal. She went through an eight-month trial as the only woman out of eleven leaders of the Soweto Students Representatives Council (SSRC) who were accused of playing a leading role in the student protest of 16 June and in the subsequent mobilization against the repressive measures taken against the protestors. Nevertheless, at the end of it she was able to defy the prison authorities and mobilize other women prisoners to resist many of the cruder forms of abuse imposed on them.

Sibongile, in the last few years you've gone through a lot of hardship. Can you tell me a bit about your experiences?

I'd prefer to talk rather about the struggle, as so many other people have gone through the same thing as I have, even worse – some have lost their lives.

*This interview was conducted by the editor by telephone from Australia, September 1983.

Maybe I should then ask you how you see the struggle in Azania.

As I see it, the struggle is not merely a battle against the ideology of apartheid. It is an ideology which even whites no longer believe in. The question is whether we could, as black people, put all our efforts into such a struggle along with groups such as the Progressive Federal Party.[1] We cannot align ourselves with such groups. We have only to look at history to see that the struggle is one for land. The 1913 Land Act legalized the removal of land from the Africans and the exploitation that went with it. As a result of the Land Act, we are still struggling for land, against colonialism, racism and capitalism. The demand is for usage of the land with all that accrues from it going to all Azanians, both white and black.

Are you saying that the proceeds from land usage should be distributed to both black and white?

I am referring to the future, since this is not possible now. We do not as yet have access to the land. It is in the hands of the whites.

When did you first become politically aware?

As a child one is exposed to abnormality. I had always heard my mother complaining about whites but did not clearly understand why. What was even more confusing was that the history we were taught at primary school contradicted what I was taught at home. At home we were taught to respect our customs and uphold traditions, whereas at school these customs were portrayed as those of barbarians. I also heard my elder brother[2] talk and I became very interested. When I was in high school I could identify more clearly with the struggle. I attended Naledi High School in Soweto and in 1975 joined the South African Students Movement (SASM). It was at this time that I took the decision that I will fight until Azania is totally liberated. I felt I could identify with the Black Consciousness philosophy.

116

What is it about the Black Consciousness philosophy that attracted you to it?

At first everything was not very clear. We all knew that we had this hatred for whites because of what they were doing to us. When SASM made the call to students to fight the inferior education system and for the creation of a spirit of self-respect and pride in being black, I joined and became active immediately. Even primary school children responded. I became General Secretary of SASM.

The national uprising in 1976 (better known as the Soweto disturbances) was a significant milestone in the Azanian struggle. You, among others, played a very important role which ultimately led to your being detained, put on trial and imprisoned. What were the issues and how were they tackled?

The forced introduction of Afrikaans[3] as a medium of instruction in African schools was definitely not the only issue. It was the whole corrupt education system. Black students were venting their anger against this particular aspect because they realized that as long as the system of education lasted, the oppressed would be in the same position. We were, therefore, directing ourselves at the whole educational system. I must say that by then all students were aligning themselves with Black Consciousness and there was no question of white participation. We even discussed this issue at our conference after 16 June. It was decided that we could not include them in our ranks for the simple reason that they are our oppressors and cannot at the same time participate in our liberation. There is no such thing as a poor white. They have a choice. Everything is in their favour – laws, voting, job protection and welfare. There is then no basis to identify with us. They can appear to move to our society but we cannot trust them, as they can hop back. We do not have that choice.

Could you tell me about the Soweto Students Representative Council?

The SSRC was formed in August 1976. SASM had up to then been the student body co-ordinating activities. Although

117

there was up to then also a lot of spontaneous actions taking place all over the country, it was felt that more co-ordination was necessary.

SASM set about it this way: two representatives of each school in Soweto were to be nominated on to an umbrella body. Its main objective was the total eradication of Bantu Education. Once this decision was taken there was no going back. Similar bodies were formed in other parts of the country. The SSRC set about mobilizing the community. Trial action committees were formed to mobilize the community around the numerous arrests that were taking place. Then stay-aways-from-work, which were very successful, were organized. The SSRC continued this type of close co-operation and mobilization with workers, high-school students and university students until it was banned in 1977. Other Black Consciousness organizations, such as the South African Students Organizations (SASO) and SASM, remained very directly involved in the whole campaign until they also were banned in 1977. In fact, SASM used SASO's constitution and just adapted it for high-school students.

The sense of direction and determination displayed by these young people and their allies was remarkable and very inspiring to the black cause. The foreign white minority regime, however, did not appreciate this and detained several of the prominent organizers. Others such as Tsietsi Mashinini went into hiding for fear of their lives.

When those detained were brought to trial more than a year later, the publicity surrounding the trial and the charges levelled at the defendants made it one of the most spectacular trials. It came to be known as the Soweto Eleven Trial. They were charged with sedition, alternatively with conspiring or with participating in "terrorist" activities. (It should be noted that none of the accused were found in possession of firearms or with attempting to take any person's life.) The indictment comprised two hundred pages. It was alleged among other things that they were members of the SSRC which on 16 June and thereafter held gatherings which led to confrontation with police. Other alleged offences were murder, arson, violence, destruction of government property to the tune of 8.5 million Rand,

118

forcing people to stay away from work, the making and distribution of petrol bombs and teaching others to make them. Sibongile was the only woman charged. I asked her to recall her experiences during the detention, trial and imprisonment.

At the time of my detention I was for security reasons not at home as I knew they were looking for me. They then took away my younger sister, who was seventeen years of age and five months pregnant. They ultimately found me and I was taken to a police station in Protea, a suburb near Johannesburg. Members of the riot squad – and these are the worst bastards – asked no questions, simply kicked and beat me till I lost consciousness. The police later came and interrogated me about my involvement in the uprising. I totally refused to answer any question and they said because I'm stubborn they'd keep me in detention. I do not know how long I was in the cell.

I tried to make a complaint to the magistrate about the beatings but the Criminal Investigation Department (CID) guy who was supposed to take a statement from me instead threatened me with a gun if I made the complaint. I was transferred to John Vorster Square, where I was kept in solitary confinement for three months. I came out knowing the Bible from Genesis to Revelation, as it was the only thing you were allowed to read. I was warned that if I got involved again I'd be detained for a long time or killed, but I continued.

Shortly afterwards, I was detained once more and shifted from Protea to Viljoenkroon in the Free State, then to Vereeniging, then to Jeppe and finally to John Vorster Square until the trial in September 1978. All this time I spent in solitary confinement with only one extra dress and no soap. The police also tried to get me to be a state witness but failed. When I was told at the trial that we were being charged with sedition I didn't understand what it meant and the funny thing is that the policeman charging us didn't know either! We were all taken to Johannesburg station. They didn't allow me to stay with other female prisoners throughout the trial from

September 1978 to May 1979. I was sentenced to four years in prison, two suspended. I was relieved at my sentence because I prepared myself mentally for worse, not that I thought I did anything wrong but I have seen other people getting sentenced for doing nothing.

Although solitary confinement can be a terrible experience, I found prison conditions worse. It can make or break you. I decided, though, it was not going to break me, nor dehumanize me. For instance, they gave us overalls, from which there was a change only once a week. I'm not a pig; so I walked around in my panties and bra in protest. We were then given denim overalls thrice a week.

The food always contained either flies or cockroaches. In the two years I spent in prison I went on three hunger strikes. On the first occasion it lasted for eight days. We were charged in prison, with the warder presiding, with disrespect because we refused to get into our cells. With the third hunger strike, we were taken to court on the fifth day and convicted and sentenced to fifteen days' spare diet. Now the spare diet is a system of punishment instituted by the internal prison court. You are not given food at all for five days, then for the next five days you are given only dry saltless porridge, and the last five days the porridge with a bit of vegetables. We continued our hunger strike, regardless.

We were then transferred to Klerksdorp where we were seen by a doctor. After the eighth day of our hunger strike he pronounced us fit to go on the spare diet! So many things happen to you in prison that if it doesn't break you nothing will. I was due to write my matriculation exams. I applied and they agreed but when the time came I could not go because I was charged. I'm due to write my last three subjects in October 1983.

Sibongile was released from jail in May 1981. The South African State was determined to inflict more suffering on this courageous woman. They served her with a two-year banning order, which restricted her to one area, forced her to communicate with only one person at a time and prevented her from being quoted in the media, entering a library or any educational institution. This meant great personal hardship for Sibongile. At the beginning of 1983 she married Ishmael Mkhabela, the publicity secretary of the Azanian People's Organization (AZAPO). She could not fulfil her role as newly-wed bride by going to live with her aged mother-in-law, as required by African societal norms. Her in-laws lived outside the area she was restricted to. Nor was she permitted to visit her own parents during the two-year period.

Despite all this, Sibongile in 1982 opened a legal advice office, funded by the Witwatersrand Council of Churches, in a church building in Zola, Soweto, where she gave legal advice on the numerous influx-control laws that govern the lives of black people, and assisted those with social problems. How did she view this work in terms of her overall aim regarding the struggle?

I became increasingly frustrated with merely dealing with issues related to influx control and wanted to broaden the scope of my work. Groups such as the Black Sash do not fight the actual laws but fight the clerks who are not carrying out the laws properly. I wanted to do more than this and shifted my focus to labour issues.

Are you presently working with any group? Which other groups are active?

Yes, I'm a member of AZAPO though I've not been as active as I wanted to be in the last year or so due to my banning order. I'm also a member of Black Women Unite (BWU). The Azanian National Youth Unity (AZANYU) and the Azanian Students Movement (AZASM) are very active and have the support of not only high school and university students but the black community as a whole. This is because all three organizations involve themselves in community affairs whether these be unfair rent increases or fighting the forced removal of black people from shanty towns. AZANYU organizes black youth in general, and the newly formed AZASM is essentially a student body mobilizing black students at high school and university.

What is your view regarding the position of women in the African struggle for liberation?

It is the aim of the Black Consciousness Movement to get black women to participate fully in the black liberation struggle. Women still tend to shy away because they associate the struggle with prison and see it as only for men. It is much better, I think, for women to organize other women. They need to be slowly incorporated in the struggle and will be a force to be reckoned with. The organization Black Women Unite was formed to mobilize all black women throughout the country. AZAPO at its last congress reaffirmed their position on women and stated that they do not see women as exclusively women but as part of the black community. They must therefore participate as equals alongside black men.

The interview was now finished and Sibongile had to see to her two-week-old little girl Ntsako. I asked her whether she had any special hopes for the future of her daughter.

I'm hoping that she'll be brought up in a free society and will not have to go through what I and her father are going through.

NOTES

1. This was up until recently (1985) an exclusively white parliamentary party whose platform is a qualified franchise for certain categories of black people, such as those with a certain level of education.
2. Kehla Mthembu, a former president of the Azania People's Organization (AZAPO) and one of the leading proponents of Black Consciousness.
3. A patois spoken by the Dutch segment of the settlers in South Africa.

III: Zimbabwe

Introduction

Zimbabwe's hard-won liberation has not only altered in a physical manner the balance of power in Southern Africa in favour of the indigenous Africans in the region, but has also psychologically buoyed those still fighting colonialism and settler-colonialism in Namibia and Azania. It has demonstrated in very practical terms the efficacy of the armed struggle and the inevitability of victory over colonialism. Mugabe's Zimbabwe has for Africans on the continent and in the diaspora the same significance that Nkrumah's Ghana had for them at independence in 1957 and throughout his rule.

The country of Zimbabwe formed the centre of the once powerful empire of Mwene Mutapa. The states comprising this empire have been involved in diverse economic activities since roughly 300 BC. Mining of iron, gold and tin, for example, took place on a large scale: old mining sites attest to this. This era was marked by vigorous trade, not only among states in the empire but also across the Indian Ocean. Gold was the main export. Ironware processed in the empire was also in great demand in India by 1200 AD. Skilled architects built beautiful cities of stones with magnificent temples. Some of these decayed with the passage of time; others were destroyed by the invading Europeans. Some, like the remains of Great Zimbabwe, survived as evidence of the level of affluence and technological advancement of Zimbabweans prior to European occupation.

The colonization of Zimbabwe and the first Chimurenga[1] war is discussed earlier on in this book (pages 56–8).

The two interviews with Zimbabwean women provide an illuminating glimpse of the harshness of life for Africans during colonial rule. Reduced to slaves in their own country, they were subjected to atrocities which will leave physical and emotional scars for a very long time to come.

The second Chimurenga war was launched by the Zimbabwe African National Union (ZANU), the ruling party, in 1966. ZANU was formed on 18 August 1963 in the house of Enos Nkala, the present Minister of Home Affairs, after it broke away from the Zimbabwe African People's Union (ZAPU). It was not until nine years later, however, in 1972, that what is termed the "decisive phase" of the armed struggle commenced. This was a well planned, brilliantly executed guerrilla war, commencing with the attack on a settler farm on 21 December 1972 by a unit of nine ZANLA[2] guerrillas. The Rhodesian army was well equipped and backed by the South African Defence Force. It carried out severe reprisals against the rural population, whom it accused of harbouring the guerrillas. This often took the form of getting to a village where they suspected guerrillas were active, assembling men, women and children at random and gunning them down in cold blood.

The Rhodesian army on numerous occasions also violated the sovereignty of Mozambique and indiscriminately bombed camps housing exiled Zimbabweans. One such attack, the most bloody, took place on ZANU camps at Chimoio and at Tembwe in Mozambique in November 1977. These camps had some military units but were mostly civilian. Chimoio was an administrative centre with a hospital, school, food and clothing stores. More than one thousand people were killed. They included hospital patients, school children and women. Despite these attempts to destroy ZANU the party were to bring the Rhodesian army and settler state to its knees, militarily and politically, seven years from the date of the commencement of the decisive phase of the armed struggle. ZANU victory at the polls (fifty-seven of the eighty parliamentary seats for Africans) of the British supervised elections was a mere formality. ZAPU, whose forces had done a small percentage of the fighting, mostly in the south of the country, won twenty seats. Britain's Thatcher was bitterly disappointed. Apart from encouraging the retention of twenty parliamentary seats for her kith and kin, she had hoped that ZANU would be swallowed up among the myriad of parties, thus neutralizing any outright victory. Journalists had already confidently predicted that ZANU would win at the most thirty-five seats. Sharing her disappointment was the Soviet Union, America, Western Europe and anti-apartheid movements in Western Europe and Britain, all of whom to a lesser or greater degree supported Joshua Nkomo's ZAPU party exclusively. Besides the African countries who supported ZANU there were also China, Yugoslavia, North Korea, small but well-organized solidarity organizations in Western Europe and Britain, and of course African people in the diaspora.

Having regard to the recent history of Zimbabweans, it should be a source of amazement to freedom-loving people everywhere that someone like Ian Smith should today sit in parliament unharmed, instead of being put on trial for the crimes he committed against the African people. This show of magnanimity on the part of the Zimbabwean government has apparently not been appreciated by Smith, who still exhibits his contempt for Africans in general and the Zimbabwean government in particular by his frequent racist outbursts when travelling abroad.

The unmistakable and widespread support for ZANU during the war and at the elections make the Zimbabwean government one of the most legitimate governments in the world. Yet this has been ignored by Western governments who have attempted to undermine it. A massive media disinformation campaign was launched against Zimbabwe soon after it became clear that ZANU won the British supervised elections in April 1980. This campaign, carefully stage-managed in the best traditions of a Hollywood drama, complete with carefully arranged skeletons in "mass graves" supposedly dug by the Zimbabwean government, has been partly successful. It was planned in the capitals of a hostile Europe, the United States and South Africa, angry because their horse did not make it to the winning post. While it is probable that some of the journalists involved in this campaign are intelligence agents, the rest are simply displaying their typically European contempt for anything and everything African. Moreover, Zimbabwe has the potential to become a strong and prosperous African nation, for historical reasons totally independent of the East/West superpower rivalry, and therefore one of the few truly non-aligned nations.

The tactics employed in this campaign involve:

— the highlighting and exaggeration of political differences and reducing them to ethnic differences or "traditional tribal hostilities", as well as ignoring or down-playing positive achievements of the Zimbabwean government and people;
— the spreading of outright lies like the so-called killings of civilians by government troops;
— innuendo and distortion, as was the case with the reporting of the role of one of the Zimbabwean army units, the Fifth Brigade, in combatting armed bandits.

The aim of the campaign is two-fold. It seeks to:

— wage economic sabotage by discouraging any confidence in the viability of the Zimbabwean economy, thus hampering foreign investment and frightening away tourists (an important source of foreign currency);
— curtail, on the one hand, the positive effect of ZANU's military victory over the white settlers on the morale of Africans in Azania and Namibia and, on the other hand, to boost that of the whites who are not prepared to accept African rule in Zimbabwe.

The lack of information in the South African and Western media regarding the considerable achievements of the Zimbabwean government in its first five years is directly attributable to the above campaign. Below is a brief summary of some of the notable advances made by the Zimbabwean government in its first five years.

In education, the colonial regime channelled virtually all resources to settler children and placed numerous obstacles in the way of African children gaining an education. As a result, at independence only 40 per cent of primary school children were enrolled. The first major step was the introduction of free and compulsory primary education in 1980. The percentage of children now attending primary schools has risen from 40 per cent to 93 per cent. Enrolment, which stood at 819,586 pupils in 1979, has now risen to 2.5 million. This pattern is repeated in secondary education. At independence there were only 177 secondary schools with 66,215 pupils. There are now 1,129 schools with 422,584, a growth of 538 per cent.

Racist élitist education was abolished when the government abolished exclusive white schools which barred African children, a common feature of colonial Rhodesia. Sex discrimination in subject selection has also been abolished in schools, as well as in teacher training colleges. Many girls are, therefore, now doing courses previously reserved for boys. Each teacher, male or female, who graduates should be able to teach one technical and one academic subject.

But the most profound change surely needed in any postcolonial education system is the decolonization of the content and orientation of a system which sought to glorify Europe and European achievement and degrade Africa and African achievement. This cannot be accomplished overnight. The government is aware of this problem and so far a review of the curriculum has taken place up to Form Two. Great emphasis has also been placed on the teaching of science. ZimSci (Zimbabwe Science) kits, designed by Zimbabweans at a lower cost and educationally superior to its imported equivalents, are used with great success at secondary schools, even remote ones where science could not previously be taught due to the lack of electricity. Other countries in the region, among them Botswana, have been so impressed with the results of these kits that they have imported them for use in some schools in the country.

At independence, an acute shortage of teachers existed in

view of the ambitious expansion programme. Large numbers of foreign teachers, mostly European, were recruited. Though keenly aware of the cultural risks involved, the government saw this as an interim measure until they have trained enough Zimbabweans. The output of qualified secondary-school teachers annually is now five thousand as compared to one thousand prior to independence.

Another area of crucial importance is that of rural development. Its importance arises from two things. First, the majority of Zimbabweans are peasants who live in the rural areas. Secondly, it is they who carried the liberation war on their shoulders. As a result of this, they were subjected to the brutality of the Smith regime. Whole communities were unceremoniously uprooted and dumped in concentration-like camps guarded by the Smith army, the so-called protected villages.

In recognition of the above, the government set up the Ministry of Lands, Resettlement and Rural Development. Various programmes have been implemented by this Ministry to make the rural areas viable economic zones. On independence, large communities were resettled on arable farming land which, in accordance with the Lancaster House agreement, the government had to buy from settler farmers. To date 21,109,480 hectares have been bought at a cost of $50,652,192 (Zimbabwean). Co-operatives were then formed to farm and develop this land. Some of these co-operatives have done quite well in the production of food and cash crops. Assistance and advice is also given to small-scale farmers. These government-assisted small-scale farmers in 1984 produced record maize harvests which in themselves were enough to feed the whole country. Zimbabwe was able then, despite having gone through three years of drought, to export to Zambia some of the surplus maize by other producers such as the co-operatives and commercial farmers.

Small-scale farmers were successful because for the first time they had access to credit facilities, technical advice and assistance, all of which were previously available only to settler farmers.

The Position of Women

Zimbabwean women have the potential to set a shining example to the rest of the world as to the meaning of true female equality. Their major role in the liberation struggle has made them acutely aware of the obstacles in their path. It has also made them assertive in their demands for equality. It is to their advantage that the ruling party ZANU, as well as the government, is committed to not only granting legal equality but also to sanction programmes geared towards educating Zimbabweans about the need for the full participation of women at all levels of society. Prime Minister Robert Mugabe in particular is a staunch ally of the women. In 1984, the Legal Research Department of the Ministry of Justice, Legal and Parliamentary Affairs completed a review of all statutes in force in Zimbabwe, with a view towards repealing or amending them with regard to women. At a conference hosted by the Ministry of Community Development and Women's Affairs in November 1982 the Minister of Legal and Parliamentary Affairs, Dr E.J.M. Zvobgo, said: "I have already stated that the Government does not need to be persuaded about the need to bring about the full equality of women with men. We have an interest in this which is not only born out of our war experience but is selfish. Women are a vital link in our chain of national development and if they remain behind and weak, our total effort to that extent will be slowed down."

Furthermore, various ministries and organs are constantly involved in the organization of seminars, conferences and interministerial debates concerning the status of women, always in consultation with the Ministry of Community Development and Women's Affairs. Several statutes and subordinate legislation have been enacted for the benefit of women. These include: the Legal Age of Majority Act of 1982, which gives women full contractual capacity and freedom from parental control on reaching the age of eighteen; the Equal Pay Regulations, which outlaws discrimination against women in the workplace and ensures equal pay for the same kind of work; maternity leave regulations which provide that women can take up to ninety days' maternity leave without losing their jobs or career prospects; the Sex Disqualification Act, which gives Zimbabwean women the right to vote, to hold public office and to participate fully in politics and public functions.

The Age of Majority Act has had a tremendous impact on Zimbabwean women and society as a whole. It was one of the first steps the government took to honour its commitment to women. During colonial occupation of their country, Zimbabwean women, like their counterparts in South Africa, were subject to "customary" law used for the same reasons as in South Africa. They were therefore perpetual "minors" subject to the guardianship of their father, brother, uncle and husband. The Act abolishes this guardianship after a woman has reached the age of eighteen. A woman can now own property in her own right. She can marry without parental consent.

In the landmark case of John Katekwe *vs* Mhondoro Muchabaiwa,[4] the provisions of the Act were for the first time interpreted. At issue was a father's entitlement to damages for the seduction of a daughter who was a major. John Katekwe appealed against a decision of the Community Court for the Province of Midlands, which ordered him to pay the father, Mhondoro Muchabaiwa, $800 (Zimbabwean) for having sexual intercourse with his daughter, who was a virgin at the time. The daughter was aged twenty when intercourse first took place in May 1983. The Supreme Court upheld Katekwe's appeal. The effect of the ruling is that women over the age of eighteen, the age of majority, can sue for seduction damages in their own right. It furthermore makes the paying of lobola (bride price) on marriage optional, as opposed to compulsory. The prospective bride can decide whether she wishes to marry with or without lobola.

It was after this decision that the Act became quite controversial. Women and those men who support their fight for equality hailed the decision as a major victory and a correct interpretation of the letter and spirit of the Act. Other men, mostly a small but very vocal urban élite with access to the media, have adopted a hostile stance towards legislation of this type, under the guise of preserving "tradition". This opposition arises from a low political consciousness which in turn can be due to the fact that these men played little or no role in the war of liberation. The controversy particularly relates to the payment of lobola, a practice grossly misrepresented by Europeans and abused by present-day African men. Some academics also argue that certain provisions of the Act are ambiguous and need clarification. It is not intended to get involved in this debate here except to state that if indeed this is the case, legislative amendment and judges can attend to this problem.

The controversy generated by the above Act is in a sense a microcosm of the reactions that now and in future will surface in response to women pressing for and the government reviewing, amending and abolishing laws which discriminate against women. Many problems remain. Not least of all the poor representation of women on decision-making bodies. However there has been a significant improvement. The Minister of Community Development and Women's Affairs, Ms Tuerai Ropa Nhongo, a dedicated and determined spokesperson for women in Zimbabwe, recognizes that a lot remains to be done. Her ministry has decided to set up a "women's desk" in more or less every ministry in the government in an attempt to "spur government ministries to action in the cause of women's advancement".[5] The reaction by the various ministries to this exercise has been mixed. As women are not a group on their own but rather an integrated part of society, an integrated approach is necessary. "Some laws, for example, the labour law, the income tax and the criminal law could not be replaced overnight because they require a lot of detailed research and consultation. Others like these laws which affect our traditional values will require a lot of persuasion before they can be changed."[6]

Despite these problems, for Zimbabwean women equality is

a reality. There is a vigorous campaign by the Ministry of Community Development and Women's Affairs to spotlight problem areas and set about solving them. On the basis of research, they formulate recommendations on changing laws and practices and co-ordinate with other ministries to see that the legislation and measures adopted are implemented. It also co-ordinates the activities of women's groups, at both a national and international level, with the work of the ministry. This includes the dissemination of information, assisting women's groups to identify local needs and resources, directing development groups to areas of need especially in rural areas. Forums are organized to discuss women's legal rights and to raise consciousness through existing women's and community networks. It provides aid to women's groups in the form of technical assistance, training service and financial assistance to approved projects.

In the coming years the process of consolidation of political and economic independence and reconstruction in Zimbabwe will be keenly observed by Africans at home and abroad, who will find it a source of sustenance. If the first five years is to be a measure, African women in Zimbabwe will increasingly play a powerful role in this process.

NOTES

1. Liberation war.
2. Military wing of ZANU during the liberation war.
3. *The Government of Zimbabwe, 5 Years of Achievements*, published by the Ministry of Information, Posts and Telecommunications.
4. Judgment No. SC 87/84.
5. Extract from a speech delivered by the Honourable Minister to the Public Service Association on 25 January 1984 in Harare, reproduced in *Community Action* magazine (published by the ministry).
6. Edson Zvobgo, Minister of Justice, Legal and Parliamentary Affairs, in an interview with *Moto*, a Roman Catholic publication (October 1984).

Women and Decision-Making: The Case of District Councils in Zimbabwe*

Ruvimbo Chimedza

The type of development that occurs in any given area depends, to a very large extent, on the institutions involved in the implementation of the development programme. Regardless of the different ideological beliefs and proclamations made by politicians, the origins or historical development of those institutions determine the type of development that takes place. For instance, the lopsided type of development resulting from the contradictory characteristic of capitalist development of expropriation and appropriation evident in underdeveloped countries is perpetuated in the post-independence era, even in so-called socialist countries. Furthermore, sexual and racial biases are part and parcel of this contradiction, which exploits one group of people and benefits another. It is therefore important to note that in analysing problems of women, one needs to look at them within the broad context of the world economic system, because the liberation of any oppressed group of people cannot be separated from economic liberation.

This paper looks at roles of some institutions in the development process and how they relate to women. It attempts to critically examine these existing institutions, with the aim of recommending ways in which they can enable

*This paper was prepared for the conference "Women and Institutions in Southern Africa: Strategies for Change", hosted by the Ministry of Community Development and Women's Affairs in Zimbabwe. It took place in November 1982 in Harare, Zimbabwe.

women to participate more effectively in the process of development. The study focuses on district councils which are Zimbabwe's decision-making and planning authorities at the grassroots level. It will analyse the way in which various district councils have involved women in their development programmes, in an effort to determine whether there need be any changes that will enable women to participate more effectively. In conclusion, the study will make recommendations based on the investigations and explanations in the text.

The question of women's participation in the process of development has recently received a lot of attention from social scientists, activists and politicians. A loud cry for integrating them into the social, cultural, political and economic development has gone out and various governments and development agents are responding in different ways. To date, however, very few genuine attempts have been made to change the situation of women. Attempts made by most underdeveloped countries have not been effective at all. In fact, most countries have only tried to improve the situation of women without changing it. The few efforts that have been made to change the situation have been thwarted by the fact that governments continue to use the same institutions that were designed to benefit the metropole to the detriment of the peripheral countries. The terms "metropole" and "periphery" will be used to describe the developed or industrialized countries and the underdeveloped or non-industrialized countries, respectively. The institutions excluded a larger part of the population from benefiting from development, because they responded to the needs of the metropole countries.

Although most underdeveloped countries are now independent, the situation has not changed much. The historical development of these countries clearly shows the creation of economic dependence on the part of the peripheral countries. The role of peripheral countries or colonies was to produce raw materials for the manufacturing industries of the metropoles. They produced agricultural products and minerals which were shipped to the metropoles for processing into their final forms, some of which were sold back to the peripheral countries. The main aim of the metropoles, or companies from there, was to maximize profits by minimizing costs. They did this by paying low wages to their labourers. In the majority of cases those wages were just enough for the subsistence of the employee but not his family. Furthermore, male labour was preferred to female labour, partly because companies found it more economic to leave women with the full responsibility of reproducing labour without any cost to them. In other words, companies or colonialists did not contribute towards the reproduction of labour in any way.

> Because even the scanty social services were meant only to facilitate exploitation, they were not given to any Africans who were not directly producing surplus for export, to the metropoles. That is to say none of the wealth of exploited Africans could be deployed for the assistance of their brothers outside the money economy.[1]

These companies or colonialists, however, found it advantageous to create a small local bourgeoisie which helped perpetuate the system. A few local males were co-opted into the government structures, forming a new class within the indigenous population. This group grew as foreign investments expanded and it served to facilitate the new economic activities. At the same time, this local bourgeoisie acquired the tastes of settlers and therefore provided a market for luxury goods that had to be imported from the metropole countries.

Although male local bourgeoisie benefited by having some access to education, experience in bureaucratic and managerial skills, women in this class did not have the same opportunities. Their participation was not favoured in many areas except in the fields of teaching and nursing. In one of Boserup's earlier studies, she concluded that:

> In most countries, two-thirds or more of all women in the professions are teachers and a large proportion of the

137

remaining one-third are nurses or perform other medical services.[2]

These areas did not give power to women. They were not involved in making decisions or effecting change. Even in the fields of teaching and nursing, women did not occupy decision-making positions, such as being principals or hospital administrators.

In the area of finance, women hardly had a role to play. They did not have access to credit and unfortunately this was supported by governments through constitutions and laws. Women were regarded as minors for the whole of their lives. They therefore could not borrow from financial institutions without their husbands or male relatives acting as their guarantors; in fact, it was more desirable for the male relatives to borrow on behalf of women. In rural areas women did not hold title to land. Where there was a scarcity of resources, priority was given to the education of boys. Such biases were apparent throughout the society.

To date, at a time when more than 90 per cent of former colonies are independent, the situation has not changed. Underdeveloped countries are experiencing a certain amount of development, with women still lagging behind. In fact, in progress, the gap between men and women is increasing. The local bourgeoisie has taken over the leadership positions in politics, government bureaucracies and even managerial positions in foreign companies. In most cases, these local leaders just moved into these positions without changing the structure in favour of the development of their countries, and the rest of the neglected masses, in particular women. These institutions are still functioning to exclude women from fully participating in the development process so that they continue to reproduce labour at very little cost to governments.

The above information has aimed to explain the present situation by briefly analysing the historical developments that took place to exclude women from the development process. It has looked at the problem within the context of a capitalist system, with special reference to colonialism.

What follows is a case study of specific institutions in a given area – and how they relate to women. It is an attempt to present evidence to the above data and make concrete recommendations for change. The case study will look at district councils in Zimbabwe and how they relate to women.

Historical Background

The political economy of colonial Zimbabwe was characterized by the dispossession of land of the Africans by settlers. The gradual alienation of land, which eventually stripped the Africans of the most fertile soil, resulted in the country having three categories of land, i.e.:

a) farms and mines sometimes owned by European farmers or in the hands of absentee landowners and companies,
b) crown land, unalienated land, which was regarded by the ruling British South African Company as its own until a Privy Council decision confirmed it as belonging to the British Crown,
c) reserves, set aside for the exclusive use of Africans.

It is category (c) that this paper is mainly concerned with, because this land carried the majority of the African population, particularly women. By the late Seventies, just before independence, about six thousand white commercial farmers owned 40 per cent of the total land area or 46 per cent of land outside urban areas. Only 42 per cent of the total land area (or 54 per cent of land outside urban areas) was in the hands of rural Africans who constituted about 75 per cent (5.5 million) of the total population, estimated at 7.5 million. This African rural population occupied the most unproductive land with a poor physical and social infrastructure. Of the total rural population, at least 75 per cent were women, mostly engaged in subsistence agricultural production.

One fundamental role of the land category (c), reserves later known as Tribal Trust Lands, was to provide cheap male labour for the settler's economy. This, to a large extent, explains why the percentage of women in the rural areas is very high. The low wages paid to these male labourers accounted for women's involvement in subsistence agriculture. Furthermore, controls discriminating against the marketing of the African agricultural produce were firmly established.[3]

The Maize Control Act of 1931 limited African agricultural production and marketing activities because it allocated a very small marketing quota to the majority of the farming population and offered them lower prices than those given to European farmers. Since most of the able-bodied African men were being coerced into working on the mines, industrial areas, and European commercial farms, women who remained in the rural areas were hit hardest by these discriminatory laws and control measures.

The rural population continued to suffer, partly because their interests were ill-represented at all levels. District commissioners, who were all white, were responsible for the administration and development of reserves. Functionally, their major responsibility was to protect the interests of Whites by acting as watchdogs over the rural population. They also ensured the enforcement of certain Acts governing the rural population: for instance, they settled disputes of land rights.

After UDI in 1964, two hundred African councils were established throughout the country and all their members were Africans living in Tribal Trust Lands. These councils were established by the Smith regime to promote separate fragmented development. Although African councils were the local authorities, they were not effective, partly because they had no planning authority and still operated under district commissioners. They therefore did not determine policy.

One of the major features that characterized African councils was the establishment of beerhalls as sources of income. In almost all cases this was the council's first concern.

Their concern with development programmes was not significant except in the area of education, where they had to take over the running of some of the former church schools and the distribution of books and stationery. Very little was done in the area of community development and, therefore, the involvement of women in council work was not great.

With the attainment of independence in 1980, African councils were dissolved and fifty-five district councils were established. These new councils, made up of elected political representatives, were charged with the overall responsibility for development in the former Tribal Trust Lands, now known as communal areas.

District Councils: Situation, Functions and Responsibilities

District councils cover all communal lands and some purchase areas that decided to join. At present, 95 per cent of district council land is owned communally and the rest is privately owned by the black small farmers.

At their formation, district councils were charged with the overall responsibility of the development of their areas. They are the decision-making and planning authorities responsible for all reconstruction and development. In short, they set conditions for all development. In implementing their development plans, they may seek technical expertise from other service ministries or departments such as the Ministries of Construction, Water Development and the Department of Physical Planning. Generally, district councils are responsible for the provision of such services as health-care centres, primary and secondary schools, roads, clean water, dipping tanks, posts, improved agricultural services, public order, recreation, building, equipping and letting business premises, facilities for milling and shelling produce, social centres or community halls, undertaking marketing projects, etc. One of the most significant functions of district councils is to organize people for self-help projects, particularly for the construction and reconstruction of schools and health-care centres. At present, district councils are responsible for a total of 395 hospitals, 286 co-operative marketing outlets, 2,915 primary schools and 539 secondary schools (Control Statistics, 1982).

The Participation of Women

Although women comprise approximately 75 per cent of the total rural population, their participation in decision-making is insignificant. In the majority of district councils, women are not at all represented, despite the fact that councillors are elected to office. The biases in favour of men are a function of a number of factors. Political parties that field candidates for district council elections tend to favour men as opposed to women. This is a reflection of the whole political system. Women's representation in the party leadership is insignificant. Therefore, their interests are not well represented; for example, the ruling party, ZANU-PF, whose Central Committee numbers about 33, has only three women. ZAPU presents a similar picture. This lack of women representatives at leadership level is clearly reflected at grassroots levels by an almost total exclusion of women. This is, however, just a symptom of the problem. The basic problem is the whole capitalist system, which links with some cultural traditions to exclude women from the process of social, cultural, political and economic development.

The process of socialization for Zimbabwean women elsewhere has been such that they hardly speak out in the presence of men and seem to vote for a male rather than a female candidate. This is partly the result of those colonial practices which excluded women from taking the leadership role and exploiting their potential, particularly in the modern sectors of government.

Of course, the attitudes of some male politicians also provided the right climate for the continuing exclusion of women. Although Zimbabwe went through a war of liberation, in which men and women fought side by side, such biases have been perpetuated. They were reflected in the sexual composition of district councils in 1981. The following figures illustrate the point. For convenience the different regions will be divided into three: Region I, comprising fifteen district councils, has 424 councillors, 11 of them female; Region II, comprising eleven councils, has one female councillor out of a total of 240 councillors; Region III, comprising twelve district councils, out of a total of 321 has only three women members. The situation has not changed much since.

Although women are virtually excluded from decision-making, when it comes to providing labour, particularly in self-help projects, they make a very significant contribution. For example, in the construction and reconstruction of schools and health-care centres, women are responsible for making the bricks, fetching firewood for baking them, water for mixing cement, grass for thatching, preparing food for all those working and in most cases they carry children on their backs while they do all this work, yet when councillors are determining where and when the schools and health-care centres are to be built, women are not present. In a situation where the provision of clean potable water is recommended, for instance, women who are responsible for fetching water, cooking and laundry are not always consulted as to the location of the boreholes or pump, whatever the case may be. The same applies to community centres, which to a large extent are predominantly used by women's clubs and various women's organizations. In fact, most of the services provided by district councils are more frequently used by women than men: when children fall ill their mothers take them to the health centres; when there are social or political gatherings at community centres, women are always in the majority. It is the women who are responsible for most of the laborious preparations for such gatherings.

In cases where males are away working in the modern sector, women represent their husbands at family, social and school functions. It is quite true that many women in the rural areas carry a double burden. They play the role of provider for the family, raise their children, till the land and still fulfil their social and political obligations. Women continue to reproduce at no cost to the capitalist in industry, manufacturing, mining and even government. They work hard under very difficult conditions but they are still marginalized. Their contributions, although very vital to the economy of the country, in both the modern and traditional sectors, are hardly recognized.

The case of district councils is a good example of the almost total absence of women in decision-making, even at a grass-roots level. This implies that these vital institutions may not be effectively representing the interests of the majority of the population who understand their own problems and sufferings better than anyone else. The sexual composition of district council members seems to suggest that these institutions have not changed much since the colonial era. A case in point is that of beerhalls being one of the major income-generating activities of district councils. This has been inherited from the colonial African councils, which did not carefully assess the social costs and benefits of encouraging the establishment of beerhalls as one of the major sources of income. In fact, a lot of resources have been concentrated on this type of investment which in itself does not generate any development in the rural areas. It drains labour from agricultural activities by attracting men who often spend hours drinking while women are busy in the fields or marketing commodities.

The area of marketing is a crucial one where women should be consulted prior to any decision being implemented. Marketing activities in rural areas are dominated by women, not only in terms of agricultural produce but also of farm products such as crafts. The majority of rural women are engaged in various income-generating activities which involve marketing. In most cases when district councils make policies relating to marketing – for instance, of crafts – they may not even be aware of the fact that if a dyed piece of crochet work is kept in the sun for too long the colour is spoiled.

Normally, district councils do not have the time and resources to carry out research before they make policy. One can therefore assume that decisions are made on the basis of their experiences and the knowledge they have acquired in the course of their lives. In Zimbabwean society, there are a lot of things that men should not know about because they are meant for women only. In fact, most men look down upon some of these women's issues. The same is true for women who may get elected. It is therefore essential to have both sexes represented.

The above discussion clearly shows that the district councils, responsible for the development of rural areas, need to be changed so that they effectively service the special needs of the majority of the population. It is clear that although there has been some restructuring, with independence, the functioning of these institutions and their biases have not changed much, particularly where women are concerned. The exclusion of 75 per cent of the rural population from formulating the development programmes is likely to have negative effects on the implementation of such programmes.

Notes

1. W. Rodney, *How Europe Underdeveloped Africa* (London: Bogle-L'Ouverture Publications/Dar-es-Salaam: Tanzania Publishing, 1972), p.226.
2. E. Boserup, *Women's Role in Economic Development* (London: Allen & Unwin, 1970), p.125.
3. UNCTAD, *Zimbabwe, Towards a New Order: An Economic and Social Survey* (New York: United Nations, 1980), p.12.

Interviews with Teurai Ropa Nhongo and Ntombelenga Takawira

The following two interviews were conducted in April 1980 by an Azanian, Lindiwe Mimi Tsele. They were done just after ZANU had comprehensively won the British-supervised elections, and speak volumes about the suffering African people, particularly women, endured at the hands of white settlers. These and other interviews were collected in a booklet entitled *Zimbabwe Women in Chimurenga* (Black Women's Centre, London, 1981).

Teurai Ropa Nhongo (née Mugari)

Teurai Ropa Nhongo was ZANU's first Secretary for Women's Affairs. She, like thousands of other African boys and girls, men and women, left the then Rhodesia in 1973 to join ZANU. Her commitment, dedication and leadership qualities made her rise in the ranks of the liberation movement. She underwent military training and thereafter became medical assistant, then Military Commander and Central Committee member and finally Minister of Community Development and Women's Affairs in independent Zimbabwe, a post which, due to her experience in the liberation war, she is eminently qualified to occupy.

Teurai is all life, vivacious and full of carefree laughter.

My parents were peasant farmers at Mt Darwin. I was the middle child of nine – three brothers and six sisters. I went to school at Howard Institute in the Mazowe area. There was nothing special about my schooling. It was like that of any

146

other Zimbabwe child except that by around 1973 we had ZANLA forces speaking to us about politics. On returning to college we experienced more conflicts with the white staff because what they wanted us to accept was in almost total opposition to what the ZANLA forces had maintained. It was inevitable that we should fall out with our college authorities. It was these restless months that finally encouraged me and several others to leave school and join the ZANLA forces in the bush. We did not stop to think about our parents. When I ran away with the others both of my parents were still alive. My father only died last year.

I was collected as one woman in fifteen male comrades to Lusaka. We stayed with Comrade Tongogara for six months, after which we were sent to train as light infantry. We learned to use AK rifles and sub-machine guns etc. All this took us about three months. Later I was promoted to the General Staff, which was the first level of leadership, and became a medical assistant, training on the job for another six months. We were then given further political instruction and finally, around 1975, I was promoted to political instructor. In 1977 I went to Mozambique as a commissar and became a member of the Central Committee. Things were moving quite fast in those days and we had a lot of setbacks. One of the main ones was the death of Comrade Chitepo and Silas Shamiso, together with a Zambian child who was innocently standing near Chitepo's car when it blew up in Zambia. There were very many deaths . . . or shall we say people went missing and we could only assume them dead, such as Cuthbert Chimedza and Mudende. Before that comrade Leopold Takawira, our Vice-President, had died mysteriously in a Rhodesian prison in 1970. Many, many deaths, Sisi,* unexplained. . . . Sad things happened to us in the field and a lot of unacceptable things happened to us on the leadership side – so much so that the Party had to expel Sithole from the Presidency. His lieutenants,

---

*A term of respect for a woman of the next age group.

Gumboro Rugare, Hamadziripi and Mandizridza, also had to be expelled in 1978 after their unsuccessful attempt at a coup in Mozambique. After that they joined Sithole's party and of course lost the elections.

We had to have a Department because some particular problems facing women could not be dealt with as general party matters. I was appointed and at the same time became Military Commander of the Women's Detachment. This was a combined post, with the approval of the President and the Central Committee. In about May 1979 we had our first ever formal seminar at which Sally Mugabe, who had joined us in 1976, was appointed Assistant and Julia Zvobgo, who had returned from the States in 1978, was appointed Administrator.

We were not impressed with the appointment of only two women in the delegation sent to the Lancaster House talks, and I am sure that comrade Sally was not particularly impressed by being relegated to cooking and discussing Party matters on the return of the men from the talks.

Fortunately for us the President is much interested in promoting women whenever possible and I, as Teurai, am certain that without him our position in the Party would be in much danger.

Yes, I have children. My daughter Kumbirai Rungano was born in 1978 and my son Chipo is just eight months old. As I was a military woman in the front line Kumbirai could not, of course, be with me. I only stayed with her for one month and she then went to live with Mrs Tongogara, who is my aunt-in-law. Kumbirai naturally prefers her aunt to me – that is how it has always been in Africa. Older women, less busy outside, have always had to look after the children while the actual mothers went to work for white people.

This time I felt a very deep sense of gratification that I left my child to go to the war front to try and change all that rubbish. This does not mean that I love my child less. In fact, it is because I love her that I could leave her to go and fight in an effort to change the system that made us Africans forever slaves on the very lands of our fathers. Chipo and I stayed together for some four months, but he is really the baby of the struggle and was brought up by our comrades. He does not pine for me, which I feel is very satisfactory, because he has all these comrades for company and to him I am simply that extra special person who is sometimes around but mostly sleeps together with him.

The Chimurenga babies were brought up by comrades in Maputo, both men and women. The tradition of women only looking after babies was broken down. What with women commanders during the raids? That was a very good experience for our men as it broke down their male domination over us. Talking about those raids. Of all the raids, the one at Nyadzonia on 9 August 1976 was particularly serious. We lost between eight and nine hundred comrades. Young people – none of them over 25 years. Oh, it was pathetic to see those dead bodies of five-, six-, and eight-year-olds. . . . Smith's soldiers came in disguise and we thought they were our comrades, as they were painted black, wore Frelimo uniforms and carried Frelimo flags. They also brought with them the traitor Nyathi.

Nyathi was first one of us, then he defected to the Rhodesian side. As an ex-commander he had access to key positions – and, mother: that day Africa died, I tell you! Nyathi blew his whistle and all the comrades came out to welcome him. Nearly the whole camp was wiped out in cold blood, the trucks ran over people and those injured were shot individually because they were thought to be pretending to be dead. The massacre was horrible, worse than anything that anyone could ever have imagined about death or ever wish to see in real life or on the screen. Just a horrible nightmare. The ones who escaped to tell the tale were those who had been late in coming out to meet Nyathi the Sellout.

For a moment this vivacious young woman became tense as she narrated the story of the Nyadzonia massacre:

So many young lives. . . . What a waste of good comrades' lives.

Teurai Ropa struggled to regain her previous state of mind, but her eyes were glazed and she spoke between sighs trying so hard not to cry. "That sellout!" was all she could repeat. Having pulled herself together and swallowed her tears, she blinked a few times and went on sadly rather than angrily:

And that Nyathi had the nerve to visit our offices here in Salisbury, not once but twice, during our election campaign. We all knew that he had been sent to provoke us into action so that Lord Soames could ban our Party from campaigning so no one lifted a finger against him, but the comrades were shaking with anger – itching, I tell you, to tear him apart alive: Since the elections Nyathi has not been seen anywhere in Zimbabwe. It is said that he has fled to South Africa. That "thing" is dirtier than the whites – that. . . . Oh, I can never find a dirty enough word to describe that . . .!

Asked how she manages to be a minister, a mother and a wife, Teurai laughs heartily.

Oh, that! I have a triple job all right, as a mother, an MP and as a servant to Rex [her husband, who is a senior commander of the ZANLA forces]. I clearly can't balance all my jobs into neat compartments, so I deal with them as they come up. All things equal, I liked medicine the best of all the work I have done so far.

She winces, however, at the idea of studying science, because she imagines that that subject is a non-starter for her. She shakes her head slowly and explains her position:

Given a chance, Sisi, I really would have liked to do medicine but my life is so busy with things that need to be done now and not tomorrow that I feel it is more important for me to be here laying down the foundations for future Zimbabwean children who must never ever be forced out of school to the front line as we were by the conditions set out for us by the Whites here.

Ntomb'elanga Takawira (née Dube)

Widow of the late Leopold Takawira, Vice President of ZANU, who died in prison in Rhodesia in 1970, Ntombelanga is now a Senator.

I went to Senka Primary School at Pfungautsi (Mistry Area), which has became known as Felabusi to rhyme with the English language and their usual mispronunciation of all our names. Later I went to Hope Fountain Mission in Bulawayo, did my nursing training at Nene Mission Hospital and eventually went to work at Gogwe Hospital in Bulawayo as long ago as 1953.

I visited Salisbury as a young nurse on holiday and met Leopold, who was then a school principal in Mhofu government school here in Highfields. We got married in 1955 and soon after he resigned and started working for an insurance company. Personally, I think that was how he saw in the raw the unacceptable conditions to which so many people were subjected.

I worked as a relief nurse in the Highfield Clinic, and as an outpatient nurse at Harare Hospital and later full-time as a theatre nurse. As we were so terribly short of doctors we had to do jobs that were really way beyond any nursing training. This semi-doctoring was only relieved when we had a few white doctors who had come from the North Avenue Black Hospital in Salisbury. Our first black doctor was Dr Parirenyatwa. I can not tell in words just how much his presence meant to us and our patients. We felt so rich; it was such a good feeling to have him around. He was a real doctor, not only in medical skills but the way he treated people. His bedside manners were superb. Not only was he good with the patients but with us as well. All workers were simply thrilled to work with him, ancillary workers and all. He made you feel that your job was important at whatever level you were. It was really an experience to have a man of that kind at a time like that. We were really very lucky to have him. In 1957 we had Dr Psqarai, and with two doctors we felt that we were really running a hospital instead of the former makeshift outfit we had had, where we had been compelled to be suturing and doing things we all knew we should not be doing. But in the absence of a doctor, what do you do? You can't just stand there!

In 1958 I had my baby and became a housewife completely – and in 1960 another baby. Money was always short, so that when Mrs Victoria Chitepo asked me to give her a hand in their shop at Machipisa in Highfields, I was pleased to accept. In April 1961 I left to join my husband who was then representing ZAPU in Britain. Those were the days before the split which let to the formation of ZANU.

In Britain I met a lot of African women from all over Africa which was an eye opener in more ways than one. Africa Unity House at Earls Court in London was a building paid for by Nkrumah's Ghanaian government for all African politicians to work from. One meeting there that I will always remember was attended by Dr Nyerere, Mzee Jomo Kenyatta and Oginga Odinga. All three of them gave speeches that really lifted our spirits, but the rift between Mzee Kenyatta and Odinga was clear to all of us.

On the whole, I think I was relatively happy in Britain, apart from the fact that I was mostly alone because my husband was always out lobbying, fund-raising, etc. There were also upheavals in the Party that unsettled us all but the hope of a better tomorrow never left us. As I had no relative or anyone to help look after the children, the Party members who dropped in from time to time gave me invaluable help with the children, babysitting so that I could go out shopping or attend some fund-raising function. I will never be able to thank them enough, because without them I would have been completely housebound, a terrible thing that looks so unreal from here, where children are not such a punishment. Without everybody giving me a hand I would have had to carry the babies everywhere.

The West Indian women were marvellous, too, holding house-parties to raise funds to help African struggles. All this whirlwind was only for a short ten months. We then had to return to Rhodesia and, of course, as soon as we landed Leopold was promptly put behind bars. I was left there, bewildered, holding two babies and with a third on the way. Scratching my head or crying was not going to help. I knew that, because as a young bride one used to cry and cry and cry but as time went on you knew you needed all your strength to help you to get on with life. So my head stood still as I felt the pain going through my whole body like an electric shock. I kept dead calm, listening to all my senses.

Survival, then, was a problem. Everybody was so kind, it is unbelievable, and yet the pain of Leopold being behind bars would not go away, no matter how I tried to ignore it. In the end the Party gave me a job at their Co-operative Shop in Salisbury, where I was grateful to work until the very last Friday and gave birth the following Monday. It seems incredible, but it did happen just like that. There was really no room for tears, the poverty and the pain of all was not for crying; our tears had gone dry. Without money everything was a problem and it still is. A bit of food for us, some rent money put together. Clothes were a luxury, I simply could not afford to be fussy.

There were lots of unexplained things happening then, like passports getting lost in the ZAPU office and I had to go to and fro applying for another passport from Smith's government, leaving my young children with anyone who was humble enough to agree to do the unpaid job. There was just general ill-feeling all over. Things were really working up to the final split between ZAPU and ZANU in exile. Leopold had left prison and gone straight to Dar-es-Salaam as one of the ZANU members. In the meantime we had our houses stoned by staunch ZAPU supporters and the Rhodesian police did nothing to protect us.

That house-stoning was a real traumatic experience, especially when it became clear that the police had been instructed to leave us unprotected. Later Leopold called me up to Zambia so that he could see the baby. We did not stay long in

153

Zambia, just a few days, and Julia Zvobgo and I were promptly sent back to Rhodesia as the men went up to Tanzania to announce the birth of ZANU, which had been formed on 8 August 1963 in Mr Nkala's house here in Rhodesia.

On my arrival from Zambia in 1964 I went straight back to nursing full time, leaving the children with my cousin Gertrude Mabhunu, who was schooling in Highfields. She was marvellous, fetching them from the crêche in the afternoon while I took them in the mornings. That was to be my life as the men had again been arrested on their way back from Tanzania. Most of us were now prisoners' wives and went through all the frustrations that go with being a prisoner's wife. I will really never be able to explain enough about the hurt and the frustrations to anyone who has not been through that kind of life. It is too much. Time and again the whole thing starts afresh. In short, I can only say that my life was like that until suddenly in 1970 Leopold died in prison, having been ill inside there without any medical treatment.

My husband's death in prison has always struck me as inexplicable because that was the only week I had not gone to see him. The officials said he was a diabetic case, but diabetes does not kill people in a week! There are sugar tests and special diets and insulins that keep diabetics well for years and years on end. So that what went on in that prison during that week is a story known only to the warders and those prison walls, as dead men tell no tales.

Since then I have suffered ill health and all the doctors could say was that I was suffering from shock. Our life has really been making ends meet at the very lowest level. Ours has been that of any poor fatherless family. I have worked at Harare Hospital all this time, making ends meet as far as possible.

In 1971 the police had the cheek to come here to demand to see my husband. I was so deflated. I told them to go and ask the prison warders because I did not know what happened in that prison.

After my husband's death there was relative quiet with us in the house. Everything seemed quite dead until the big raid in

1978 when the house was half surrounded by armed policemen. I came in from a funeral and found the children playing
records and I switched off their player, pushed them into the
bedroom and thrust them to the floor. At that moment my
son, who was the only one outside, flung himself on the floor
and was missed by a shot that went through the kitchen and
landed in the middle door leading to this front room. Immediately after that the soldiers shouted that we should all come
out with our hands above our heads. We did so and they led us
to their van outside at the front side of the house. As we filed
out of the house they shot at us, hitting my daughter in the
buttock and my son just above the heart. My eldest son and my
sister's son and myself were not hurt. On their orders we all
lay there for about two and a half hours as they were still
combing the area but mainly going through our house
searching for God knows what. We were eventually taken to
Harare Hospital for treatment, where the two wounded
children were detained and we were sent home.

The very next morning the police were here asking us who
shot my children and when we said it was the soldiers the
police said that that was not possible. They did their best to
convince us that the soldiers could not be responsible because
the bullets found on the children were not those normally
used by the army! There was a special fund for "terrorist"
victims but as we would not accept that my children were
attacked by "terrorists" – which was the government's name
for freedom fighters – they did not qualify for the fund and in
any case the government said that they had not been seriously
injured and therefore did not qualify for any compensation.
My children had been detained in hospital for treatment for
nearly two weeks.

After that experience, there was no holding my two sons
from finding their way to Maputo. Thousands of children had
left Zimbabwe to cross the borders to Botswana, to Mozambique, to Zambia. As it was then, the children simply disappeared like many others and you, the parent, were left
searching high and low for them, hoping to hear anything

whatever about them. It was a relief to get news that they had been seen in Maputo with ZANLA forces.

Like all parents of children that have not yet come back, I sit and hope against hope that once they had been seen in Maputo so again they might still be somewhere, perhaps with the forces that have not yet been released. But there is absolute silence which I fear to acknowledge. So many children have not come back, only God knows. . . . I too, like thousands of other families, sit here hoping and praying that with each release of the young fighters from the camps that among them perhaps, with some luck, mine too will be there. We hope that we too could be among the lucky ones.

Mrs Takawira, like all of us Blacks, simply went ashen grey suppressing the anguish of the possibility of the death of her two sons, but we both skated over what was uppermost in our minds. The nervous tension of it was only betrayed by a twitch of the nose and the rubbing together of her fingers. With a very calm voice she continued answering my relentless questions to the point where I felt I was being brutal . . . but the experiences were hers and she was the sufferer, and I felt that I had no right to put words into her life to suit whatever I was after, which was a record of the African blood that has flowed on this soil for the liberation of Zimbabwe.

After the elections, the Prime Minister Mugabe invited me and it was then that I was informed of my new post, that of Senator. The official announcement was on 11 April 1980. In the meantime, my aged mother, my daughter and myself hope that, now that our Party ZANU has won the elections, things will be better for all Zimbabweans and that the worst abuses of human liberties are over.

Inasmuch as we are all pleased that ZANU-PF has showed appreciation of my late husband's contribution during the Chimurenga days, the biggest heartache of every parent now is that of the missing children and this silence about their whereabouts. There are hundreds. We all know that a lot of children died during the raids but it is difficult not to hope that perhaps your ones, somehow, survived the massacres of

Smith. My daughter Ratitso, aged 16, is at home with me. My sons, Hamadishe ("Honour humanity", 22) and Tafirinyika ("We die for the country", 20), are still missing.

By a chance meeting in London I met one of Sunny Takawira's sons who told me that both he and his brother had survived.

And how did your mother react when you walked in?

My mother? She was too shocked. She passed out.

Why didn't you let her know somehow that you were all right?

Aunty, there simply was no time for all that. As it is, my brother has gone to Rumania without first returning home. There was no time.

IV: Namibia

Introduction

Namibia is a large and sparsely populated territory on the south-western coast of Africa. It is bordered by Angola to the north, Botswana to the east and the Cape Province of Azania to the south. It is about twice the size of Britain and has a population of about one million.

The climate is basically arid and supports dry-land crop-raising and extremely good livestock grazing. This stands it in good stead economically over and above its wealth in minerals such as uranium, diamonds, lead, zinc, copper, silver, manganese and substantial gold deposits revived in 1985/6 after a thirty-year lull. Perhaps one of the best known agricultural products from the land are the unique pelts of karakul sheep. The Atlantic coast of the territory is generously endowed with fish and other harvestable marine life, such as seals. Also, Namibian territorial waters have been confirmed to bear large oil deposits. The exploitation of these natural resources by South Africa, the occupying colonial force, has been frantically accelerated as independence has become imminent following the defeat of Portuguese colonialism in neighbouring Angola. This scramble has both been supported and joined by South Africa's major western allies. In addition, certain Eastern powers have also been documented as having practised illegal and excessive over-fishing of the Namibian coast.

The area was populated by the San and the Qhoi Qhoi from prehistoric millennia. The diversity of indigenous ethnic groups, besides these nomadic and pastoral communities, included the BaHerero, Nama, the Ovambo, the Kwanyama and the Damara. The Northern communities near the plentiful fresh water supplies of the Kunene river were the first to develop a predominantly crop-based economy. By the time of the arrival of the first Europeans in the fifteenth century, metal forging, pottery and carvings were advanced.

The frequent absurdities that colonial boundaries created is well illustrated by the pointed arrow of land that runs to the north of most of Botswana's territory and which arouses a lot of curiosity. The land, called the Caprivi Strip after the German Prime Minister of the period, was a "gift" from the British monarchy to the German colonial administration, which took possession of the territory in the 1880s. The idea was that the land would give the German administration access to the waterways of the Zambezi and other overland routes to link it with Tanzania, or German East Africa as it was called.

Colonization came after the landings of Portuguese, Dutch and British expeditions, when attempts were being made by rival European forces to find alternative sea routes to the orient other than through the Middle East. The Europeans competed for landing rights, trade and conversion of the African population to their own religions. The Germans concentrated their imperial effort largely in Tanzania, and through conquests, "treaties", purchases and other stand-over arrangements outstripped the other European powers in the primitive acquisition of the area.

Another frequent query in the discussion of European division of the area is the status of Walvis Bay. At the time of its attempt to create a dependent ethnic conglomeration run along the lines of Bantustans, the South African regime of the late 1970s declared this area part of South African territory which would not be handed over to any future administration of Namibia. Again, this was a legacy of Anglo-German bargaining during the 1880s.

The leaders of many heroic communities are well chronicled in the chapter on Traditions of Popular Resistance 1670 to 1970 in the treatise on Namibia by the South West Africa People's Organization (SWAPO). Although the Namas had fought and driven off the British landing party from the Cape in 1670, it was essentially in the late nineteenth century that European tactics became overtly aggressive in Namibia. Jager Afrikaner was the first Nama General to take up arms against the Dutch. Still, the use of traders and missionaries to extend the interests of the various European powers remained the dominant tactic, coupled with the use of the incompleteness of the process of the construction of a powerful nation state. The last mentioned fact allowed the Europeans to set up the interests of one indigenous nationality against the other.

By 1858, leaders of the BaHerero and the Namas in central Namibia came together and drew up a treaty to facilitate resistance to foreign intrusion. Jonker Afrikaner, the son of Jager, was one of the parties that drew up and implemented the treaty which lasted for only three years, but underlined the realization by Namibians that they needed unity in order to survive the colonial threat.

Several kings amongst the Ovambo, in the north, successfully pooled their forces to resist the encroachment of Portuguese forces expanding from Angola. Among these was King Kambonde of Western Ondonga, who resisted both the Portuguese military forces and the diplomatic cajolery of the German colonialist governor. Together with King Nehale of Eastern Ondonga and other Northern leaders, Kambonde even convinced the vacillating Samuel Maherero to join in what became a national uprising in 1904.

The BaHerero suffered severe losses in the battle. Samuel Maherero was able to escape with a small band of survivors across the Namib desert to Botswana. The German authorities issued and executed an "Extermination Order" against the BaHerero on 2 October 1904. This genocidal approach contrasted sharply to Maherero's own directive when he stated "women and children, non-German Europeans, missionaries, friendly traders" were all not to be harmed. Major contributions to this struggle were also made by Chief Kariko among the BaHerero and by the dauntless Jacob Morenga, who had no hereditary title and whose skills in unconventional warfare became a legend and inspiration, not only within his

Nama community but to the entire resistance in Namibia, especially after his escape from custody in the Cape Province in 1907. Resistance to colonization stretched into the first decade of the twentieth century. Only after the near annihilation of the BaHerero, the Nama and the Damara in 1907 was the control of the German occupation force complete.

The South African regime drew its claim to run the country from the fact that during the early stages of World War I when European powers battled for control of colonial territories, the British assigned the Dominion Government to serve what was then German South West Africa. The British, who had South Africa as a white dominion at the time, ordered their white subject administration to make a military takeover of Namibia. After the end of the war, the newly formed League of Nations mandated South Africa to administer the territory to "promote to the utmost the material and moral well-being and social progress of the inhabitants".

The experience of the brutal regime Germany established in Namibia made it easy for the Namibians to rally to the call of "freedom" from the British and South African forces and to rise against German colonialism in support of South African invading forces. The reality of the new colonial power, which immediately set about undermining the League of Nations mandate, made itself clear very early on. Hardly two years after its establishment, the South African administration joined hands with Portuguese occupation forces in Angola to crush King Mandume and the Kwanyama people.

The remnants of traditional resistance and leadership began to be reinforced by contemporary political movements such as Clement Kadalie's Industrial and Commercial Workers' Union, the biggest ever mass movement of Africans in Azania and other organizations, such as the pan-Africanist Universal Negro Improvement Association of Marcus Garvey from Jamaica. Repression increased in proportion and perhaps hit its lowest point of notoriety with the air-bombing massacre of Abraham Morris's and the Bondelswart's people in 1922, the same year the liberal Jan Christian Smuts ordered the massacre of African religious fundamentalists under Mgijima, when they refused to leave their baptismal spot at Ntabelanga near Queenstown in Azania. Smuts is also well known for his role in drafting the elevated phrasing of the Charter of the predominantly European League of Nations. The League of Nations collapsed in the ashes of World War II and was superseded by the United Nations Organization, formed in 1945. All mandated League of Nations territories were converted to UN Trusteeship with a view to granting them political independence. The settler regime in South Africa, however, refused to abide by this convention and set about incorporating Namibia as a virtual colony of its own.

Alongside this development there was a sharp rise of national consciousness in Namibia. World War II politicized the peoples of the colonies. As in all the colonies, the Namibian people were thrust into the cauldron of World War II, with the colonial powers championing issues such as freedom, justice and equality. Namibians were recruited for the allied forces and fought as equals alongside the white subjects of the colonial powers. These factors politicized the colonized people and made it difficult for them to be shoved back into servitude.

One of the first steps the South African settler-colonial regime attempted was a referendum to get South Africa to become the trustee for Namibia. The traditional BaHerero leaders pursued every channel to inform the newly formed United Nations that they did not wish to be incorporated under the South African regime under any pretext. Hosea Kutako and Maherero on behalf of the Herero Advisory Council asked that any referendum be conducted by the UN itself. David Witbooi on behalf of the Nama asked that Namibians be "the subject of the UN". The Ovambo and the Damara also opted for the UN, or in the case of the latter "the big nations to be the trustees".

Through the painstaking years of petitioning and protest, Namibian patriots mobilized on various fronts, particularly on the lines of trade unions. In 1957 Toivo ja Toivo and several Namibian migrant workers in Cape Town formed the

Ovamboland People's Congress which was to evolve into the Ovamboland People's Organization (OPO) and later the South West African People's Organization (SWAPO). The first organization to adopt a truly national identity is the South West Africa National Union (SWANU), which came about initially as an alliance between urban youth, intellectuals and the BaHerero Chief's Council in 1959. When SWANU was joined by several OPO leaders then its character matched its identity as a national body.

It was the implementation of South Africa's Group Areas Act in Windhoek, Namibia's major city, which first put these organizations to the test. They jointly protested against the demolition of the "old location" from where black people were being moved and "settled" under segregated conditions in the Katutura township. As often happens when harassment of communities by tyrants hits intolerable levels on bread-and-butter matters, Namibian women took the lead and marched to the residence of the South African appointed Administrator, the highest functionary of the colonial regime in Namibia, on 9 December 1967. The following day a boycott of buses and the township beerhalls were to be initiated. The location super-intendent summoned the police and the South African army. They created enough provocation by arresting and mishand-ling some of the pickets and shot the crowds as they reacted.

In April 1960, OPO was formally reconstituted as SWAPO. SWAPO took the decision to adopt both peaceful protest and armed insurrection as early as its 1961 National Congress in Windhoek. It does appear, however, that a lot of store was being placed on the intervention of the UN and the Inter-national Court of Justice which decided to sit on its hands in the 1966 hearing, rather than to make a judgement either way on the legitimacy of South Africa's continued occupation of Namibia, the abuse of its people and the grand-scale theft of its economic resources. It was not long after this non-decision that the initial skirmishes in the second armed struggle were launched in northern Namibia. The logistics were difficult and the odds were overwhelming, and until the independence of

Angola in 1975, there were problems with communications between occupied Namibia and safe rear bases in sympathetic African-ruled states; although elements of Africa's National Union for Total Independence of Angola (UNITA) appear to have assisted large numbers of Namibians to get ransit through Southern Angola in 1974, several months before Jonas Savimbi turned UNITA into a gendarme of the South African police state, for carrying out its destabilizing policy in Angola. This policy is applied throughout Southern Africa, through economic sabotage and direct military aggression by the regime often using this and other puppet organizations.

Although the decolonization of Angola gave the Namibian struggle a great amount of assistance, it would be wrong to see it as the biggest factor in the advances made by Namibians during the 1970s. SWAPO adopted an organizational form whereby the internal wing mobilized as a legal and semi-legal movement. It penetrated all strata of Namibian society and mobilized various interest groups such as students, religious organizations, peasants, workers and women around both their sectional and national needs. The external wing, on the other hand, organized the clandestine and military aspect of the struggle outside the constraints of colonial laws. It also established the most accomplished and effective diplomatic and support network of any African liberation movement.

The work of the two was interlinked and the leadership basically unified. There was a sharp escalation in all fields of the struggle a full four years before Angola's independence. On the international or diplomatic front the United Nations Security Council and the International Court of Justice (ICJ) endorsed the Namibian people's right and desire for self-determination in July 1970. A few months later, the People's Liberation Army of Namibia (PLAN), SWAPO's armed wing, carried out some of its most successful missions against the South African occupation army.

On the civilian front, South Africa was attempting to portray its puppet councillors as representing the Namibian "ethnic diversity" when they collaborated with the extension of its colonial and racial policies. They met with massive rebuffs from the representatives of all Namibia's indigenous nationalities and from the leaders of the major Christian churches and black students throughout the territory. All these forces were demanding the implementation of the ICJ decision. The repressive measures which followed only escalated the tempo and the intensity of mobilization.

The majority of workers in Namibia are victims of the South African "migratory labour and single-hostel system". They are restricted to arid and unproductive labour reserves and are not permitted to compete for work in the industrial and commercial parts of the territory. They are recruited from these reserves on super-exploitative terms by the various enterprises that run Namibia's mining, fishing, farming and transport industries. Their permits to leave the reserves are tied to their contracts to work for whichever employer transports them from the reserve. Conditions in both the company dormitories, where they stay, and in the production process are well recorded in a variety of documents by the United Nations Centre Against Apartheid in New York, the International Defence and Aid Fund in London, the Southern Africa Support Campaign in Sydney, Australia, and by various church bodies as well as by SWAPO.

Resistance to these conditions, particularly long working hours without compensation for overtime, led to the outbreak of a massive overtime-ban campaign that initially covered the fish cannery workers in 1968, followed soon by the harbour workers. Walvis Bay and Katutura townships were the effective nerve-centres of the struggles which built up over three years. Towards the end of 1971, the campaign against the migratory labour system, as an important aspect of South African colonial policy, was moving towards a general strike. This is a very effective tactic, as has often been demonstrated in Azania, in so far as it interrupts the profitable operation of imperialist enterprises. It also has inherent weaknesses, including the fact that the workers have limited resources and can only withhold their labour for limited periods. Also, large unarmed concentration of opponents make easy targets for violent disruption by the forces of the state. Lastly, even if one set of industrialists are affected very badly by strike action, they can always rally resources and raise loans, or will be replaced by equally exploitative elements of similar type. The state forces that protect them remain intact.

The national general strike of 1971/72, executed with skill and determination, apart from forcing the state to make concessions, served to galvanize the patriotism of the Namibian population. Tremendous advances were made by SWAPO during the period.

The rapprochement with SWANU (not as well known as SWAPO but nevertheless very active in the anti-colonial struggle inside Namibia) which came after the removal from SWANU's ranks of the opportunist Moses Katjunguo in 1985, is another major advance for the struggle in Namibia (see interview with Nora Chase, SWANU's Foreign Secretary). It neutralizes the one possibility the South African regime had of playing ethnic games with the people of Namibia by using SWAPO's Ovambo origins to present the movement as either regional or ethnically dominated.

Namibian Women

The history and struggles of the peoples of Africa often suffer from lack of documentation and differentiation between retrogressive and imported ills and traditional social burdens. In Namibia's case one finds a society very closely related in many ways to Angola and other societies in the region, yet there is no trace of any of the great matriarchs or women leaders who have abounded all over Africa. As more means of research (historiography, archaeology etc.) become available to the Namibian people, these heroines, who most surely existed in the territory, will be brought to the fore to take their rightful place among its national symbols. Frequent reference is made to practices and attitudes which appear to have had their foundation in Roman, Dutch, Germanic and other European practices, as being "traditional" African attitudes. Many African male intellectuals hide behind such terminology when they seek to justify exploitative behaviour in interpersonal relationships. African women also frequently submit to such arguments in order not to be seen as alienated and Europeanized.

The larger scale involvement of Namibian women in all aspects of the independence struggle is bringing a critical focus on ideas and practices which deprive or abuse women. This involvement is varied and dates back to the earliest days of the struggle. After the genocide of the Herero people by the German army in 1904–5, the women took a decision not to bear children while German rule lasted in their homeland. Later, Herero women set the pace once more by refusing, when they could afford it, to humiliate themselves by becoming "nannies" for white settler families. In 1955, women were prominent in the BaHerero revolt against the apartheid-practising Lutheran Church in Namibia, which culminated in the formation of the Oruuano, an independent community church. In 1958 it was the women who were responsible for the routing of government puppets from the Windhoek Advisory Board. They mounted a successful campaign against one boardman, Mungunda, who had asked the government to apply corporal punishment to women pass law offenders.

The women's participation, especially in organizing and combat roles, should create role models for future Namibian society. However, it often occurs that if compromise settlements are reached before such liberation struggles have affected and influenced entire societies, then the capitalist consumer-orientated and white-identified role model, which made no contribution to the struggle, retains its dominance as the ideal woman. A deliberate cultural reorientation is essential for the changing of such attitudes. Such a change will not follow automatically from the fact of the advance of the anti-colonial, anti-imperialist struggle.

NOTES

1. *Namibia: The Crisis of U.S. Policy towards Southern Africa*, a pamphlet by TransAfrica (Washington DC, 1983).
2. Department of Information and Publicity, SWAPO of Namibia, *To be Born a Nation* (London: Zed Press, 1981).

Biography of Lucia Hamutenya*

As SWAPO's Secretary for Legal Affairs, Lucia Hamutenya has gained first-hand experience of the widespread repression and torture suffered by people in Namibia.

Lucia was born in 1952 in Odibo in northern Namibia. She grew up in a family committed to SWAPO. Her father had been detained and interrogated about SWAPO in the early 1960s, and had been flown to Pretoria, South Africa, by the South African security police in 1967 to testify against Herman ja Toivo and thirty-six others then on trial under the Terrorism Act. He was released after two months, having refused to give evidence. Her brother fled the country in 1962 after protests against Bantu Education. Lucia attended political rallies from childhood and experienced police brutalities at demonstrations and meetings.

She attended secondary school in Windhoek and studied law at Fort Hare University in South Africa. She is one of a tiny number of Namibian women to have a university degree. She was expelled from Fort Hare University and forced to return to Namibia in 1976, when the Soweto uprising resulted in the closure of many schools and universities in South Africa. She completed her studies through a correspondence course with the University of South Africa in 1979.

Lucia, who had joined SWAPO in 1968, started working at the SWAPO national headquarters in Windhoek in 1976, organizing the defence of political detainees and raising funds

* This biography is taken from To Honour Women's Day (International Defence and Aid Fund for Southern Africa, in co-operation with United Nations Centre Against Apartheid, August 1981).

for bail and to assist the relatives of detainees. She was active in mobilizing support for SWAPO, especially among Namibian women, going from house to house, handing out pamphlets and addressing rallies. She travelled widely throughout the country, helping to organize demonstrations and meetings. She was detained for several days in December 1977 at a military camp in Oshakati and questioned about SWAPO's guerrilla activities.

Virtually the entire SWAPO leadership inside Namibia were arrested in April 1978. As the only member of SWAPO's national executive still at liberty, Lucia ran the SWAPO office and informed the press about harassment and threats against SWAPO supporters by the DTA.

On 3 December 1978, on the eve of South African-sponsored internal elections in Namibia, Lucia was among a large number of SWAPO officials and members to be arrested. She and others were picked up in early morning raids following a demonstration in Windhoek against the elections, where police had beaten up people and taken many to police stations. Her attempts to obtain their release were halted when she was herself detained under the Terrorism Act. She was made to stand in the centre of a room while being questioned about her work in SWAPO and her connections with SWAPO officials in Angola. She was slapped in the face and suffered damaged eardrums as a result. She and other SWAPO leaders were released on 23 December 1978.

During 1979, Lucia was detained twice. Her longest period in detention began in April 1979, when she was detained under Proclamation AG26, together with many other SWAPO officials, and held in solitary confinement at Gobabis prison. During her detention, Lucia was exposed to psychological pressures during interrogation, resulting in hallucinations, nightmares and fainting spells. She was unable to eat or sleep. She was transferred to Windhoek Central Prison after her condition had become serious, but continued to suffer from hallucinations and nightmares. Although she was seen regularly by a doctor, she was only given tranquillizers.

173

After her release from detention on 27 July 1979, Lucia continued her political activities. She organized a rally for Namibia Day on 26 August, attended by more than thirty thousand people. She travelled to the north of the country, collecting evidence about the disappearance of SWAPO supporters and taking affidavits on torture from victims and their relatives. At the end of 1979 Lucia left Namibia for exile after further police harassment and questioning.

Interview with Nora Chase*

Nora, could you let us have some biographical information about yourself?

Certainly, but there is not much. I was born on 1 December 1940 in Windhoek. I was married to a man from the Caribbean who could not live within the apartheid society of Namibia. He went back to the West Indies and sued for divorce two years ago. I have three children, two girls and one boy, all living with me. I am the Director of formal education with the Namibian Council of Churches. I am also the Secretary for Foreign Affairs of the Politbureau of SWANU.

I understand you spent some time overseas some years back. When did you return to Namibia?

I returned to Namibia in 1978 under the amnesty which was granted under UN Security Council Resolution 435. I was at the time elected Secretary General of SWANU and worked full-time in the party headquarters for one year. Thereafter, I joined the Namibian Council of Churches in the position I am presently holding.

Could you briefly outline the present situation in Namibia?

Since 1978, South Africa has been paying lip-service to

*This interview was conducted (by telex) from Gaborone by the editor, with Nora Chase in Windhoek, in January 1986. A day before the interview the office of the Namibian Council of Churches, where Nora works, was burnt down. Arson was suspected. So the interview had to be conducted in the offices of the Lutheran Church.

acceptance of Resolution 435. In respect of South Africa it must be borne in mind that they do not follow one single strategy with regard to Namibia. Despite protestations to the contrary, South Africa has been trying repeatedly to put obstacles in the way of the implementation of Resolution 435, while at the same time trying to create an anti-SWAPO front. Its latest endeavour with the Multi-Party Conference (MPC)[1] is just another attempt to create a situation of relative calm inside Namibia so that it can concentrate its efforts inside South Africa itself. The situation at present, while not having reached the dimensions of South Africa, is certainly very tense, with people deciding not to take the intimidation by Koevoet[2] and the police lying down. At a rally this weekend (January 25) the crowds for the first time fought back when they were attacked by the police.

What are the chances of success of the interim government set up by South Africa?

The so-called interim government has no chance of success for two main reasons. The first lies within the MPC. The MPC could only have stood a chance of some success if it were in a position to make some changes in the status quo, i.e. to remove A.G.8 which entrenches apartheid and tribalism. If you look at the parties in this unholy alliance, you will immediately see that the Nationalist Party will never accept this situation. Despite statements of intent and declaration of human rights, it is obvious that all this is only on paper and there has been no change, for example, in the security legislation in this period. It is clear that the parties have committed themselves in secret agreements to retain the status quo.

At this point power is cut and we cannot continue. A few minutes later it comes back. When I enquire about the origin or reason for the cut, Nora simply says it is the "usual problem". She continues:

The second reason lies outside the MPC, with the people. This government has got absolutely no legitimacy. There was no election and the people do not want it. You have to consider the situation where a number of people, some of whom have no political following, are chosen by the colonial power to represent its interests and given the limited trappings of power in addition to the enormous salaries and benefits and are then a government and imposed upon the people of a country. The only reason why this so-called government can operate is that the South African Army is protecting it. Obviously, a lot of propaganda will be geared toward showing progress but in reality the only thing that has improved is the living standards of those who sold themselves to serve this so-called government.

In early 1985 there was much publicity around a crisis within SWANU which resulted in a split within SWANU. What caused this split?

I must make it very clear that there is no split in the party. It has been evident for a number of years, that the inclusion of SWANU in any interim anti-SWAPO arrangement was crucial for South African plans. The last time this was made clear was when the former Administrator General proposed a new State Council. Most of the parties in the present "interim government" agreed to participate but when SWANU refused the whole idea was scrapped. It was obvious to us that the South Africans will do everything to get SWANU in this time. They started working on a number of key people whom they knew were power- and money-hungry enough to grab any opportunity. This group included the former president of the party and a few been-tos [Africans who have lived abroad in Western countries]. They tried to expel some of us whom they knew would not collaborate but the SWANU Congress reinstated us and demoted them. They are only using the name of the party for the reasons mentioned above. They do not have the membership. In short, the whole problem was one of an internal class struggle, with the petty bourgeoisie opting to work with the oppressor.

Could you say a bit about the People's Consultative Conference set up in November 1984?

The name People's Consultative Congress was not well understood by all concerned and as such was dropped. What is more important is the decision taken by the organizations to work together to speed up the independence struggle. These organizations are SWAPO, SWANU, Damara Council, Mbanderu Council, the National Unity Democratic Organization, the Progressive Party, and the Namibia Independence Party.

What are the chances of SWANU merging with SWAPO?

There is no discussion at this point of a merger, since experience has shown us that it will end up in more talk than action. What we are pursuing is unity in action with every group retaining its identity.

What are the problems faced by Namibian women?

Women in Namibia are oppressed by the system of apartheid. They are also oppressed by their traditional societies and they are their own worst enemies in that they allow themselves to be dictated to by their men. More that 70 per cent of black families are single-parent families and by that I mean the mother has to take care of all the children. Over and above that, very few men support their children and women are reluctant to use the apartheid courts, as they see them, to solicit legal assistance in obtaining support. It is common for a woman in her early thirties to have about six children from various men. With the bad socio-economic situation for blacks, it is very common to let the girls leave school and send boys ahead.

In your view how can these problems be solved?

All these problems can only be resolved as part and parcel of the national struggle for liberation. It is my opinion that we are bringing up irresponsible men in that we do not, as women, create a situation to make our men share responsibilities in the family. Conscientization of all men and women is the absolute prerequisite for a change in the situation.

What legal disabilities do black women suffer? Are there different laws for white women, for example relating to their ability to sign contracts, etc.?

According to the South African law of man and wife which exists in this country, African women cannot become legally mature. She is the ward of her father or husband. A woman who is the bread-winner of the family cannot enter into a hire-purchase agreement without the endorsement of her husband. This, of course, does not apply to white women. Married women who work are the highest taxed in the country. It seems the idea is that they belong at home and should be punished for not doing so. (In the so-called Cabinet, by the way, there is not a single woman.) One can marry in or out of community of property and, if there is a will, a wife can inherit her husband's estate. In most cases, however, so-called customary law is operative and a woman will have to go to court to fight for her rights. This, of course, in a country where most women are ignorant of these provisions or if not, lack the money to go to court and in addition are afraid of being ostracized if they go ahead.

Does SWANU have a programme for women?

Yes, SWANU does have a programme for women which is part and parcel of the party's total programme. There is a SWANU Women's League and we see it as the place where women can learn to take up leadership roles, to gain enough experience and courage to take up positions in the regional and national leadership. Over and above that, conscientization is very crucial. The women study the programme and policy of the party and other liberation movements. They learn about the struggles of other oppressed people and are further involved in Community Development Projects.

179

From your own experience as a woman involved in the struggle, what would you say are the attitudes of male comrades towards you?

It has been a long struggle at the top. Very often the comrades would expect you to do the typical women's things, like writing the minutes, cooking for party functions and serving them. In all fairness, I must say that they have internalized the question of their superiority to such an extent that they are not aware that they are trying to oppress you. They also believe that a woman's emotions dictate her political stand. Unfortunately, there have been many female comrades who acted that way. What has made it easy for me in SWANU is that it is a very democratic organization with very progressive policies and constitution. Whenever I am driven into a corner or feel exploited or oppressed I take out the constitution and the comrades are scared of violating their own constitution. I must admit, however, that one has to be very strong as a woman to insist on your rights. Also, there are some female comrades who remain subservient even if they are in a leadership position. With regard to the membership, I have always had the respect accorded to any leader who observes the leadership code and with my comrades both in the politbureau and central committee, I sometimes think we have reached a point where they see me as a comrade rather than a woman, the way I see them.

Literature on Namibia contains nothing on women in its pre-colonial period. Are there no outstanding women in the pre-colonial history of Namibia?

As you may well know, very little has been written about our pre-colonial history. Through oral tradition, though, a little is known about women during the early days of colonialism. One notable example was the wife and comrade of Jacob Morenga. She accompanied him to the Great Korras Mountain to which he escaped with some of his followers in a spectacular manner, despite a large-scale offensive by the Germans to capture him. One day he called his small group together, told them that he was the person the Germans were after and that he could no longer see them suffering because of him. He told them that he was going to surrender. When he did so the following day he was gunned down in cold blood. His wife, thinking he was dead, took the baby off her back, handed it to one of her daughters and walked towards her husband. She was shot and killed, and when Jacob saw this he forced himself up but was shot again and again. They were buried together. One cannot mention the heroines of the colonial struggle. They are so many. If one only thinks of women who were tortured and raped by the Germans and who still trekked through the Kgalagadi Desert carrying their babies or being pregnant. They even ate scorpions just to remain alive and feed their babies.

Notes

1. A coalition of parties all committed to maintaining South Africa's hold on Namibia, unilaterally installed as an "interim government" in early 1985 by South Africa, in violation of UN Security Resolution 435.
2. Officially known as the South West African Territorial Force (SWATF), it is a unit of the occupying South African Defence Force set up to fight SWAPO guerrillas. It has become notorious for its indiscriminate killings and torture of innocent civilians.

Biography of Rauna Nambinga*

Rauna Nambinga's experiences illustrate the harsh manner in which the South African police and army treat civilians in Namibia.

Rauna, a trained nurse who was born in 1950 at Okadiva in northern Namibia, was twice arrested, in 1975 and in 1980. Each time she was tortured, ostensibly for giving medicine and money to SWAPO guerrillas. She described her experiences to the International Commission of Inquiry into the Crimes of the Racist and Apartheid Regime in Southern Africa, at its meeting in Angola in January 1981.

On 17 September 1975 Rauna was working at Engela, a Finnish Mission Hospital, when she was arrested by members of the South African security police and taken to a detention centre at Ogongo. Her arrest took place at a time of large scale police operations against SWAPO members. Rauna was interrogated for seven days by police, who asked her if she gave medicine and money to SWAPO guerrillas. When she denied this, she was beaten with rifle butts, exposed to the sun for long periods, and hung from the roof by a rope tied to her arms behind her back.

She was transferred to Ondangwa prison on 24 September 1975, where her ordeal continued. She was kept in solitary confinement in a cell which contained one blanket and a bucket. She remained there until the first week in November,

*This biography is taken from To Honour Women's Day (International Defence and Aid Fund for Southern Africa, in co-operation with United Nations Centre Against apartheid, August 1981).

and was called once or twice per week to the office for further interrogation. Each time she was beaten and forced to agree that she had helped SWAPO guerrillas. From Ondangwa, Rauna was transferred to Windhoek Central Prison where she was held in solitary confinement throughout November, sometimes without being given food or drinking water for three days at a time.

On 1 December 1975 she and five other SWAPO members – Aaron Muchimba (SWAPO Treasurer and National Organizing Secretary in Namibia), Hendrik Shikongo, Andreas Nangolo, Naemi Nambowa and Anna Ngihondjwa (the last two also nurses from Engela Hospital) – appeared before the Windhoek Supreme Court charged under the South African Terrorism Act with being members or active supporters of SWAPO and taking part in "terrorist activities aimed at overthrowing the lawful administration of South West Africa". Rauna was accused of crossing into Angola to meet a group of SWAPO members and giving them goods and money. Called to give evidence, Rauna told the court that she had joined SWAPO in 1973 after attending a meeting at Engela that had stirred her. She found that SWAPO rejected apartheid and the homeland policy and stood for a single unitary state. It was fighting for the interests of the people and for Namibia's liberation. Rauna described her crossing into Angola with her brother to distribute food and goods to people who had fled across the border to escape from the effects of apartheid, floggings and repression.

On 12 May 1976 she was sentenced to seven years' imprisonment. Death sentences were imposed on Shikongo and Muchimba. Rauna was transferred to Windhoek prison at the conclusion of the trial and later to Kroonstad Women's Prison in South Africa. Serious irregularities were discovered in the conduct of the trial, however, which led the Appellate Division of the Bloemfontein Supreme Court to set aside the death sentences and to cancel the prison sentences. Rauna was released and returned to work at Engela Hospital.

She was again arrested on 15 July 1980, taken to Oshakati

prison and asked to give details of assistance given to SWAPO. She was again severely tortured, given electric shocks and hung by a rope from the roof. She was beaten so severely by police that a doctor at the military hospital found that her head was seriously injured, her eardrums had burst and her left kidney was also injured. She continued to be tortured, subjected to assault and attempted rape.

On 10 November 1980, she was taken to Swakopmund and told to work in a supermarket. She was regularly visited by the police, and pressured to act as an informer and agent. She refused. On 24 December 1980, Rauna decided to run away from Swakopmund, and succeeded in making her way to Angola. In January 1981, she gave evidence in Luanda to the International Commission of Inquiry. She told the commission that she was still unable to hear properly with her left ear, that her head remained numb and that she had continual pain in her ribs and chest on the left side.

V: Botswana

Introduction

Botswana is a big country. Its land area is approximately 577,570 square kilometres. It has a population of approximately 1 million and is completely landlocked, and therefore heavily dependent on South Africa for its supply lines.

Archaeological diggings show that by 650 AD, in the central district of Botswana, a large farming population had settled on the upper Motloutse river stretching southwards to Shoshong. The inhabitants built quite large villages on hilltops, with smaller settlements scattered around them. They kept large herds of cattle, smelted iron and grew crops. The diggings also confirm the presence of the San and Qhoi Qhoi much earlier than that. Pottery remains found near Lobatse in the South and near Molepolole, about fifty kilometres from Gaborone, and several other sites throughout Botswana, indicate that these areas were inhabited by Africans around 500–700 AD, who were engaged in the mining of iron ore, smelting, the raising of livestock and planting crops. A close study of the movements of different groups from this period onwards in the Southern African region will reveal their interrelation and effect on each other in the development of technology, and later the building of empires. The borders that exist today, of countries such as Botswana, Zambia, Namibia and Azania, are very recent developments forced upon Africans by European occupying forces in a rather illogical manner. In many instances on the continent, this practice has given rise to strife and debilitating border disputes.

Missionaries arrived in Southern Africa in the eighteenth century. In their sweep through the subcontinent Botswana was not to be spared. Here, as elsewhere, they were to act as the advance guard of the European colonists. Their tactics were the same. The first task was to learn the language of the people whose minds they were after. Secondly, they tried to convert the king or leader to their religion and assumed that his subjects would follow suit. Thirdly, they nearly always had a close relationship with traders and colonial administrations. They were thus able to obtain valuable items such as guns and ammunition for their converts and would-be converts. This was used as a leverage to convert, and with great effect. Another tactic was to build schools and provide formal education in the belief that formal education would make the African drop his religion and culture quicker. Needless to say, at these institutions freedom of religion did not exist!

Robert Moffat was to use his ability to obtain guns and military support from one group, the Griqua from South Africa, to ingratiate himself with various groups in Botswana. He was the first missionary to score successes in the conversions of Batswana (the people of Botswana), who had strongly resisted previous attempts by other missionaries. In many instances the conversions, especially on the part of the leaders, were superficial, as they were more interested in the guns and other goods the missionaries could obtain for them than the message the latter brought.

Guns were in high demand due to the various inter-African wars in the region, but more important the much bigger and more dangerous threat from the Dutch settlers who were consolidating their hold on Azania. From about 1852 Botswana faced the problem of invasion and annexation because of this threat. This was to become a reality when the British and Dutch settlers concluded an agreement, the so-called Sand River Convention. They agreed, among other things, that the British would not ally themselves with Africans north of the Vaal river and that they would restrict the sale of arms to Africans, while the Dutch could have unlimited supplies. Armed with this commitment, the Dutch unilaterally instituted their rule over Botswana. This was rejected by the Botswana rulers and now that some of them had guns, the Dutch were not going to achieve their goal quite so easily. When Kgosi (King) Sechele of the Bakwena from eastern Botswana refused to accept Dutch control, three hundred Dutch soldiers were sent in August 1852 to put him in his place. In the ensuing battle, sixty of his people were killed and two hundred women and children were captured. But Sechele's forces killed thirty-six Dutch commandos. This was indeed a novel experience for the Dutch who had never before been fired on by Batswana.

Prior to the attack, the Dutch had demanded the assistance of other Batswana groups, but these had refused to be used against King Sechele. In retaliation, the Dutch now turned upon them. Sechele requested an alliance with the British, who had control of the Cape Province which would afford them protection. The British refused. As far as they were concerned then, the territory consisted of arid land with very little going for it and therefore not worth colonizing. The cost of administering it would have been too much. This refusal had a very positive outcome, in that the various ethnic groups inhabiting what was later to become Botswana formed an alliance to fight the Dutch. The threats and raids continued, however, and the Dutch kidnapped young African boys and girls to work as slaves on their farms in the Transvaal.

In 1876 King Khama III, leader of the Bamangwato, appealed to the British once more for "protection". It is important to note that by this the Africans were not asking to be colonized but for an "alliance of independent states" in order to ward off an external threat. But once more the British refused.

In the 1880s, however, Botswana became the focus of competing colonists, namely German, British and Dutch, as competition for economic control of the whole Southern Africa region intensified. It was an important thoroughfare to the north, i.e. Zimbabwe and Zambia, which were rumoured to be rich in minerals. Cecil Rhodes wanted this gold. Botswana had also become a valuable source of cheap labour in the diamond and gold mines of Kimberley and the Witwaters-rand. All the above made Botswana infinitely more interesting to the British. In 1884 the Dutch, in one of their numerous attacks on Batswana, killed a Briton. This drew a response from Britain.

In 1885, after refusing for twenty years and without any request this time from Batswana, Britain declared Botswana a British Protectorate. This came as a great surprise to Batswana, especially since the announcement was made to the Germans and not to them. Some leaders, like King Khama, accepted this declaration on certain conditions. These were geared towards ensuring that Europeans occupied areas well away from his people to avoid problems, and that his territory was protected against attack from the AmaNdebele in the North and the Dutch in the South. But others like the Bakwena king were resolutely opposed to this "protection". They were puzzled that Britain wanted to protect them at a time when there was no longer any threat and yet such protection had been refused twice when they were truly in need of it. Widely differing views on what "protection" meant were held by Batswana and the British. Friction was inevitable. One of the ways in which the British dealt with problems was to summarily remove kings who did not accept colonization and replace them with those who could be manipulated by them. An attempt by Cecil John Rhodes, with the backing of the British government, to have the whole country transferred to his company, the British South Africa Company, failed because of the resolute opposition of three Batswana kings – Bathoen, Sebele and Khama.

The protectorate administration lasted from 1885 to 1963. The most notable characteristic of British rule during this time can be summarized in one word – neglect! They only provided that infrastructure which suited their economic interests in the whole Southern African region, such as the railway linking the then Rhodesia with South Africa through Botswana. Botswana was almost incidental. In the seventy years that Britain ruled this country, it built only one secondary school and that was in 1965, a year before independence was attained. Two other secondary schools existed, both built and administered by Batswana themselves. The

Bakgatla Secondary in Mochudi was built in 1920 by the Bakgatla people at the insistence and encouragement of Regent Isaac Pilane. The Moeng College near Serowe was built in 1951 by the Bamangwato. The missionaries also built a secondary school prior to independence. The picture in other areas, such as health, was not very much different. It is often said that had diamonds been discovered before independence, the British would never have left Botswana. If this was the case Batswana might have had to fight a war to rid themselves of the British, as was the case elsewhere in Africa.

Botswana became self-governing in 1963 and a republic within the Commonwealth in 1966. After independence, diamonds were discovered at Orapa in the late 1960s; the copper-nickel mine at Selebi-Phikwe was developed, and Botswana increased its beef exports to European Economic Commission countries. These developments resulted in increased revenue for the government. Despite the neglect of the British and natural disasters, in the form of two crippling spells of drought (the second one still continuing), the government has acquitted itself quite well in the building of a sound economic base and the provision of services for the population.

Botswana's physical closeness to occupied Azania places her in a situation where the effects of unrest and hostilities in South Africa affect her security. The South African regime is embarrassed by the unfavourable comparisons which are drawn between itself and Botswana by those who favour the Westminster parliamentary government and values. It also seeks excuses for its instability by attributing the on-going uprisings, which have occurred since 1976, to refugees and persons from the liberation movements resident in the neighbouring states. From 1984, the colonial regime has been trying to induce Botswana to sign a peace treaty similar to the one they forced on Mozambique. Botswana's leadership has adopted a position whereby it acknowledges that South Africa has the military power to over-run and bully Botswana; at the same time Botswana upholds its right to retain the values it has chosen and to fulfil such international obligations as granting asylum to victims of political persecution and instability from whatever source and without regard to their political outlook. The most overt instance of South African wrath this policy has drawn was the 14 June 1985 raid on Botswana's capital, Gaborone, by commando units of the South African army. Seven South African refugees, one visitor and one citizen each of Holland and Lesotho, as well as two young Batswana women, were killed in their sleep. The Lesotho national was a six-year-old boy.

All of Botswana's other neighbours have experienced similar instances of the policies of destabilization and manipulation by the colonial regime. Through raids, destruction of economic infrastructure and the sponsorship of bandit groups in Mozambique and Zimbabwe and direct incursions in Angola, South Africa is trying to surround itself with a circle of puppet administrations throughout the Southern African region.

Women in Botswana

Nearly three-quarters of Botswana's population reside in the rural areas. Women constitute 52 per cent of the overall population. In the rural areas, as in most of Africa, women are the main producers of food crops, carrying out the bulk of the tasks of ploughing, sowing, weeding and harvesting. While they are mainly involved in subsistence farming, a few such as Lesego Molapo (whose paper will be found in this book) are independent commercial farmers.

Almost half of all households in Botswana are headed by women. In the main, this is due to men having to work in the mines of South Africa for the best part of their lives. They are not allowed to live with their families. A smaller factor is the rural to urban migration which is rapidly increasing. These female heads are usually very resourceful and in both urban and rural areas ensure, sometimes under very trying circumstances, the economic survival of their families. Moreover, it is usual that in these households great emphasis is placed on the education of both boys and girls.

With reference to the legal position of women, the common law in Botswana is governed by the Roman-Dutch legal system "inherited" from South Africa. The discriminatory rules inherent in this legal system therefore also applied to Botswana, particularly the measures concerning the different marital regimes. However, the Botswana government passed legislation which radically altered the common law and greatly improved the position of married women. This legislation, the Married Person's Property Act of 1971, provides that all marriages solemnized from January 1971 are out of community. This means that a married woman suffers no legal disabilities. She is able to execute contracts, own property, sue and be sued etc., in her own right, without requiring the permission of her husband. Those couples wanting their marriage in-community of property can execute a document prior to the marriage excluding the provisions of the Act. Even those women married before 1971, without an ante-nuptial contract, can make an application to have their marital regime altered to out of community of property.

The provisions of the Employment Act have enabled women to pursue their careers and have children without fear of losing their jobs. Dismissal of a woman during pregnancy or confinement is prohibited. She is entitled to three months' post-confinement leave with 25 per cent of her normal salary. For the first year of the baby's life she is entitled to take one hour extra during the mornings so that she can breast-feed her baby. Women usually insist on these entitlements. Since independence, no discrimination in salary has existed between men and women with regard to the same type of job. Lastly, the Affiliation Act entitles unmarried mothers to claim maintenance from the father of their children and prescribes penalties for those fathers unwilling to comply with these provisions.

Notwithstanding these quite progressive legislative measures other legal, social and political restrictions remain. The taxation provisions discriminate very openly against married working women. They are taxed at a higher rate than unmarried women and married or unmarried men. They are not allowed to complete their taxation forms and cannot claim rebates and overpaid taxes. Their husbands must do it on their behalf. The taxation provisions are also inherited from South Africa, with local amendments where relevant. One statute which has recently been the subject of heated debate amongst women is the Citizenship Act of 1984. It deprives children of Batswana women married to foreign nationals of Botswana citizenship, whether they were born in Botswana or not. Children born out of wedlock of Batswana women do, however, get their mothers' citizenship, whether born in Botswana or not. These provisions have aroused the anger of women both in the government and in the private organizations. They feel that this is unwarranted discrimination, since the children of men married to foreign women inherit their father's citizenship. Women, particularly in the urban areas, have become quite a vocal and effective pressure group and with the present level of opposition from them, the provisions may well be amended. It is noteworthy, however, that in educational institutions and in the workplace there are virtually no sex-related obstacles to women providing they have the motivation and ability.

At a social level, a resilient hangover of male dominance is the false hope placed on male children as a future source of prosperity. If Botswana's skilled labour force is surveyed, a large number of women in the senior echelons of the civil service, in the professions and in some technical fields is evident. What matters more, however, is the fact that almost half of the households in Botswana are headed by women, coping very well indeed without men on both a temporary and permanent basis. Also, most unmarried young women raise their own children and contribute the main portion of their income.

A phenomenon exists in Botswana where young women are under a lot of pressure to prove their fertility before they reach twenty years of age. Furthermore, very little fatherly responsibility is imposed on men in situations where unmarried couples have babies. Although the government has provided, through the Affiliation Act, a mechanism for women to obtain support, the majority of women do not insist that the men contribute such support once their relationship is over. The situation may be due to the fact that over the last hundred years Batswana men have travelled to the mining centres and other industrial areas, mainly in South Africa and Zimbabwe, to work. The proportion of men to women at any one time has been such that when women need male company they compromise their standards and almost settle for anything. Furthermore, it is often the case that money which serves productive social processes, such as food growing, child education and home-making, comes from women's hands even where there is a male in the relationship.

When financial institutions and development organizations come to terms with the thrift and astuteness of women in handling resources in Botswana, the pace of economic and social progress there will accelerate at a pace without precedent in the country.

Interview with Margaret Nananyane Nasha

This interview was conducted by the editor in August 1983. Margaret Nananyane Nasha was at the time Deputy Director of the Department of Information and Broadcasting. She has since become the Director of the Department of Information and Broadcasting. As director, she is responsible for the only daily newspaper in the country, the *Daily News*, owned by the government, and the magazine *Kutlwano*. She is, furthermore, responsible for programming on Radio Botswana, the only radio station in the country. She also runs the Botswana Press Agency. All in all she occupies a powerful, though very sensitive, position. She is the second woman to occupy the post of Director.

Could you say a bit about yourself, your home and upbringing?

I am 36 years old. I was born in Kanye, just over one hundred kilometres from Gaborone. I am ninth in a family of ten, with four girls and six boys. My father died when I was about ten, and so we were brought up by the old lady.

I went to school in Kanye, my home village. That's where I did my primary schooling, as well as my junior secondary education. In 1967 I moved to Gaborone. I did my Cambridge Senior School Certificate at Gaborone Secondary School, after which I joined Radio Botswana as an announcer. After two years, I went to the University of Botswana. I graduated from there with English and History as my majors. I returned to Radio Botswana and worked my way up to where I am now. I look after programming and everything that goes on air. I monitor what should and should not go on air. I work with a staff that includes producers, announcers and news writers. There are both women and men amongst them. I haven't had any problems in personnel relations.

Don't you have your authority questioned by some of the men on the basis of being a woman?

No. I guess I'm a democratic person. I don't make unilateral decisions. I discuss things with my assistants. If you work this way you'll always get on well with people no matter whether they are men or women, because they feel they are part of the formulation of ideas rather than being subject to imposition of such ideas and the dishing out of instructions.

You say you also deal with the news. What does that involve?

Well, we receive most international news from Reuters and Agence France Press (AFP). The local news we get from the Botswana Press Agency (BOPA), which is part of the Information Department.

Do the international agencies give you material on Europe only, or do they deal with Africa?

Reuters is quite comprehensive. It covers a cross-section but the way we handle our news coverage is that we give priority to local issues, that is issues of Botswana, then we go on to news about the rest of our region, Southern Africa. From there we proceed to news of the rest of the African continent, and lastly news of the rest of the world, whether it be England, Australia or America. This would make up a smaller percentage than local news.

How do you face up to the complaints which African and other Third World countries have about the coverage of the major European agencies such as Reuters and AFP?

We have to put the news into a proper perspective. Obviously, you don't expect us to say abusive things about our neighbours such as Zambia and Zimbabwe. If there are suspicious reports about any of these countries from the wire services we cross-check; we don't simply put out something because it's from, say, Reuters.

Do you have the discretion to re-adjust the stories?

We have a role to play. It would be irresponsible for us to paint certain pictures of other countries when we are aware that there is a slant against African countries when it comes to these news services. That's the reason African states want to set up their own news agencies. The Pan-African News Agency (PANA) which is coming up and should be fully operational shortly, will be of great significance in this regard. [PANA is now fully operational.] It should do a lot of good and we should be able to get accurate news about other African countries.

Getting back to you personally, do you have a family?

Yes. I'm married with four kids, all boys, ranging from twelve to three and a half years old.

Do you find being a working mother and holding down a nine-to-five job a problem?

It never was much of a problem to me. We are given three months' maternity leave by the government. In those three months you can raise the baby at least through the most critical stages and then get back to work. We also have access to hired domestic help. You can employ someone to look after the kids. Also lately, the government has made it possible for nursing mothers to go home for an hour in the morning, to breast-feed, which I think is a good idea. Some people bring in their mothers to raise the baby until it's about five months and then the old lady can go back home. By that time the baby has grown reasonably big and is no longer much of a problem.

When you say people bring in their mothers, are you talking about the functioning of the extended family?

Yes. That's when you realize the value of the extended family. Your mother remains your mother. As I always say, in our society you can rely on your mother until she dies. I could be forty years old, and regardless of whether or not I'm married I can still call upon her for support. She can come and live with me in my house until both of us are satisfied that no further assistance is needed.

In the villages, I believe, sometimes when a woman has a baby she gets looked after for a period of, say, three months. I don't think that happens in the towns or cities.

Well, in the villages, when a bride or expectant woman is close to confinement she is moved from her in-laws' place to her own mother's place. There she gets looked after by her mother or her aunts, cousins, or sisters. For about four months she stays indoors and does not associate with strangers, who might be ill and might pass diseases on to the baby. That's part of our custom. At the end of this period there is a big feast where the mother and child are free to mix with people. Of course, this only happens in the traditional villages and settlements.

Could you tell us what changes independence brought to Botswana?

The situation with education and infrastructure illustrates the extent to which the colonial government neglected the Bechuanaland Protectorate, as it was then called. In the whole country there were very few secondary schools, mostly run by missions. There were very few primary schools. There was about twelve kilometres of tarred road as compared to over fifteen thousand kilometres to date. Primary health care and public health education were virtually nil.

In a way we may have been lucky. I've always said that if some of the country's rich mineral deposits had been discovered during the colonial period it could have led to bloodshed, people having to fight for independence because there is something in their land the colonial government wants to retain. They don't want to leave and they start claiming they've done all sorts of things for the country because they see a place full of riches. That's why other countries in Africa have had to fight so hard and lost so many lives for independence. On the other hand, the British government thought we had nothing worth fighting for, so it was through a process of negotiation that we made a peaceful transition to independence.

As I said, very little was done by the British during their period of rule in Botswana. They did not even build an administrative capital and were content to run the affairs of the country from South Africa.

Looking at education in Botswana, eighteen years after self-government, we now have about forty government secondary schools in the country. In addition, there are three teacher training colleges, village polytechnics or Brigades Centres, and a National Vocational Training Centre. This and the Brigades provide Batswana with their first access to trade and craft training facilities which never existed before 1963. We share a university with Swaziland, so one campus is in Gaborone and the other is in Swaziland.

The government also runs a correspondence college for workers who want to raise their educational standing through private part-time study, and there are in-service training facilities for up-grading the skills of civil servants.

Could you expand on other areas of development besides education?

Well, as far as communications go, we now have an automatic dialling telephone system linking all the towns and major villages. You still find operator-connected services in the smaller villages, but from all major centres we have international direct-dialling services. All major villages are joined by tarred roads and links between places such as Jwaneng,

Lobatse, Molepolole and Pikwe, and the main national road going north to south through the country is just about to be completed. Water is one of the great constraints on the development of Botswana. Conservation measures and underground water drilling will, hopefully, take care of this problem.

What has been the situation with health care?

Like health authorities elsewhere, Botswana's Ministry of Health is aiming for good health for all by the year 2000. Much has been done, especially in the field of primary health care. I've recently [mid-1983] produced a basic health-care radio programme, and have found that part of the Health Ministry's thrust is educating rural communities about health, with an emphasis on preventive rather than curative measures. A lot still needs to be done but I think things are moving in the right direction. Looking back we used to have so much tuberculosis (TB) and it's still common but, comparatively speaking, there's been a great improvement. At least now people voluntarily go to hospitals, because there is no longer the stigma once attached to TB when sufferers were almost social outcasts. There is now an understanding that the disease can be cured.

What role have the women of Botswana played in development work?

The women have made their contribution mainly through their voluntary organizations. These have set up projects which benefit young kids, such as establishing nursery schools throughout the country, for example.

Would this refer to organizations such as the Young Women's Christian Association (YWCA), for instance?

Yes, the Botswana Council of Women (BCW), the YWCA, the Business and Professional Women's Club and the Women's Section of the Bank Employees Union. Some organizations run courses for school-leavers and drop-outs, as well as kids with no places in the formal secondary-school system. They teach them useful skills such as typing, which could lead to jobs, or dressmaking which provides the option for self-employment. The Ministry of Commerce and Industry runs a set-up called the Botswana Enterprises Development Unit (BEDU), which assists small businesses with managerial support and training. They have a reasonable success rate.

What I'd want to make clear is that there is no legal segregation based on sex in Botswana. It is a matter of competing on merit. The problems women face are based on the fact that for a long time girls have been conditioned to believe that they cannot become anything except nurses or secretaries. Lots of women have proved it can be done. We have women doctors who run their own surgeries. Some are running their own firms as private legal practitioners and doing very well. In fact, one of the most successful practices in Botswana was a partnership started by two female attorneys. I hope more will come forward. I think, though, women still need to be told about these things; maybe a Ministry of Education careers guidance team has to either speak to kids in Junior Certificate or Cambridge School Certificate.

In politics, women have been pretty active too. We have two lady Cabinet Ministers: Mrs Disele, Minister of Home Affairs, and Dr Gaositwe Chiepe, who is Minister for Mineral Resources and Water Affairs.* We have a lot of women councillors and in the capital, Gaborone, Mrs Basadi Mookodi is probably one of the most hardworking. For a long time the Mayor was Mrs Mannathoko. The Executive Secretary of the Botswana Democratic Party, the biggest and stablest political organization in the country, is Clara Olsen.† Basically the positions are there if we work for them. I do not believe in the promotion of women into important positions only because they are women. I think it's fair that we should earn whatever position we can through hard work.

* Dr Chiepe is currently Minister of Foreign Affairs.
† Clara Olsen is now a government-appointed member of Parliament.

What's the situation with wages?

Government policy is that all posts have standard salary scales, regardless of the sex of the holder. This applies both to the public and the private sectors.

Women and Agriculture in Botswana*

LESEGO MOLAPO

It is necessary for women from rural and urban areas to meet and exchange views. I am pleased, therefore, to be able to discuss with urban women some of the problems confronting us women from the countryside. The topic of discussion will be Women's Role in Agriculture. We all know that the involvement of women in agriculture is a long-standing tradition. Way back, women used to gather wild greens, forest fruit and edible roots. I wouldn't say these have been abandoned even while some of us are now in agriculture.

Women are the people who carry out agricultural work. Starting from harvesting, it is women who preserve or prepare seeds. Since the woman prepares the food she knows what is to be cultivated. For instance, at this time of year (March) we would be eating *makgomane* [a green vegetable shaped like a butternut pumpkin], sweetcorn and melons, the things a mother prepared as nourishment for her kids.

Botswana is a developing country, with the majority of the population in the rural areas and an emphasis on agriculture. Women form the backbone of agriculture and should be recognized for this. We know that when our sons are still strong they dissipate their strength in the mines of South Africa and lately in our own country. They leave their mothers, sisters and wives behind minding the lands and the livestock. It is a fact that there are men who work alongside

* This paper was translated from Setswana by Margaret Nananyane Nasha.

204

women in agriculture but the truth is that women lead by far. Furthermore, 42 per cent of households are headed and run by women whose men are either away or deceased.

Also, when formal education started, women were pushed back, a situation which exists until today in our economy and our lives. It is only in nursing and in lower primary education where women are the majority. We have a preponderance of men in formal jobs. For example, we have male agriculture extension workers, *bo Rra lophalo* [livestock improvement officers]. It's a painful situation because they do not communicate satisfactorily with households led by women. They say they cannot go to Ms So-and-So's because they don't want to have their time wasted by the women. Yet these women need the advice of agricultural extension workers also. We shouldn't let our lack of educational standing and expertise hold us back. The rights of women in agriculture should be visible. We should develop our skills and not fall behind and blame our lack of schooling. There are many women, as I've indicated, who are carrying this country on their backs with agricultural production.

Besides restrictions in formal training, there are other methods employed to keep women backward and oppressed. There are both traditional and recent practices whereby women are discriminated against. Furthermore, there are contemporary organizations which discriminate against women, bodies such as land-boards and financial institutions. Some men find it a sacrilege for a woman to stand and address a Kgotla meeting and express her views in relation to agriculture or some mutual advice that may be shared. I speak as a rural resident, where it happens that if one raises a point as a woman, it is not properly regarded because of our Setswana tradition. A married woman does not get land allocated by land-boards for cultivation and stock-raising purposes without a letter of authorization from a male guardian. Women whose husbands have gone to work for whites in South Africa or whose husbands are absent have to wait up to six or even eight months to get such authorization.

This is, of course, very inconvenient.

Women encounter lots of obstacles when they try to borrow money. They are treated differently and feel isolated. This we see when one borrows capital for crop cultivation. A woman is required to provide security and to show that she can use the money properly. Why would we raise loans if we had such security? A woman raises loans out of being in a needy position. These things ought to be thoroughly examined by our administration, so that we as women can grow crops; yet because we have problems and men oppress us, our lands are the last to get tilled so that we may even miss the rains and our crops will fail. They will not, therefore, be of much value. Such are problems that beset us as women.

I am happy, though, that today women are aware of these obstacles and try to overcome them despite difficulties. Our government also tries to assist us with other things, such as the practice of the Kgotlas, things which men simply do although the government does not permit them.

One observes, on occasions such as agricultural shows, how women are developing expertise. They do not simply bring exhibits; they undertake the work of preparing for expected visitors and judges. It could safely be stated that women make or break the agricultural shows. To see to it that the nation is fed and nourished is a very important task. It is here that men and women should co-operate to improve the standard of living of the nation, yet this is not the case.

I'm not provoking women to get into a fight about rights. We simply want the nation to recognize their contribution. Let's go along with a government which says we should stand up and not wait for someone else's hand. There's a Setswana saying, "*Mokodue go tsosiwa o o itsosang*", which amounts to the idea that help is given to those who raise themselves up. If we speak out for ourselves and perform skilfully as farmers, as so many women have done in our country, we cannot be ignored. Let us therefore stand on our own feet!

VI: Tanzania

Introduction

The coast of East Africa was lined with trading cities engaged in a vigorous trade with Asia from the second century AD. By the tenth century, the people of present-day Tanzania exported leopard skins to Muslim countries, tortoiseshell and ivory to China and India via Oman. In turn they imported ceramics from China and Southern Persia. Remnants of these have been found on the islands of Manda, Zanzibar and Kilwa. Arab traders featured in the economic life of East Africa from about the tenth century. But Arabs fleeing from civil wars and persecutions in their homelands started coming to Tanzania, which then formed part of the Zanj Kingdom, from about 8 AD. Around 12 AD they started setting up more or less permanent residence in parts of Tanzania.

Like other African countries, Tanzania attracted the European powers. In 1885 Otto von Bismarck took the decision to colonize Tanzania. Rivalry between the various European colonizers heightened during this period; Britain was Germany's main rival for control of the region. Between 1884 and 1886 expeditions were sent by the German East African Company to make "treaties" extending its control over Tanzania. As elsewhere on the continent, these agreements were often obtained by fraud or intimidation. Bismarck himself remarked: "To acquire territory is very simple in East Africa. For a few muskets one can obtain a paper with some native crosses."

The Germans occupied Dar-es-Salaam on 25 May 1887. They also demanded that they should take charge of the customs throughout the coast. When agents of the German East African Company arrived to annex seven coastal towns, in August 1888, the Africans, who had long been dissatisfied, rebelled. The resistance in coastal towns were reinforced by fighters from inland. In September of that year, the Tanzanians gave the Germans two days to leave the country. Some escaped but two officials in Kilwa were killed. Resistance to the Germans lasted until 1890, when the local people, despite their bravery, were beaten by the superior fire-power of the Germans. Thereafter, German rule became entrenched in Tanzania and was not to be seriously challenged until the Maji Maji rebellion of 1905-7.

The Maji Maji rebellion appeared to have been a desperate attempt on the part of the colonized people of Tanzania to rid themselves of the Germans. The rebellion was significant in two respects. First, religion was used as a rallying force with great effect. Secondly, the uprising was organized across ethnic lines and was marked throughout by inter-ethnic co-operation.

In 1903 the Germans forced Arab government agents and ethnic leaders in the southern coastal districts to establish cotton plots to be cultivated communally by members of the communities. This meant the neglect of the people's own fields. They earned very little. To the Matumbi people, who lived in the highlands north-west of Kilwa, cotton was identified with foreign occupation and they were the first group to plan to shake off this occupation. But they were not a military people and only fought if they were attacked. Also, they were aware that the Germans were strong because of their weapons, and instead of a military campaign decided to uproot cotton, the symbol of their oppression.

The leader of the uprising was a prophet called Kinjikitile, who came to prominence in 1904 when he became the medium for an important spirit. He built a religious shrine to which pilgrims flocked in their thousands. His religious philosophy stressed unity and offered leadership and protection. But the most potent weapon he offered the people in their fight against the Germans was his medicine called Maji. It was believed that this medicine would protect a person against

European bullets. He set up a command system in different areas to prepare for the planned uprising. News of the medicine and the planned uprising spread and thousands came to his centre to obtain the medicine and fight the hated Germans. All that was needed was for him to give the signal for the war to commence. However, before he could give such a signal a group of Matumbi people decided, without consulting him, to uproot the cotton and so declare war. They launched an attack on a cotton farm in Samanga in July 1905 and burnt the Asian trading store. The German forces sent to investigate and take action were ambushed.

The Matumbi had retreated to the mountains and organized lookouts in the tree tops, while ambushing patrols. Kinjikitile was hanged on 4 August 1905. He defiantly announced on the scaffold that his medicine had already reached other groups. This was true and the uprising spread to the states of the Southern Highlands. Some of Kinjikitile's assistants were killed by the Germans which introduced an element of doubt as regards the effectiveness of the Maji, and contributed in the long run to the failure of the uprising.

Britain gained control of Tanzania after waging war against the Germans. This was agreed at the Peace Conference of January 1919.

The Tanganyika African National Union (TANU) was formed on 7 July 1954, with Julius Nyerere as one of the moving forces behind it. Nyerere subscribed to the principles of African Nationalism which swept the continent in the 1940s and 1950s. TANU rallied Africans around the slogans "National Freedom", "Uhuru" and "Africa for the Africans" with great success. The British were alarmed at the "radical" platform of the party and set up a multi-racial structure, the United Tanganyika Party (UTP). The structure of the UTP was modelled on the British Conservative Party and believed that only "educated" Africans should be given the vote. Foreign-owned companies donated generously to the UTP. They believed TANU to be a threat since it did not accept white

211

patronage and called TANU "black racialism". The multi-racial UTP was set up by the British to defeat the African Nationalism of TANU. TANU successfully campaigned among the population, both on the coast and inland, against European colonization and forced the British colonists to call elections in September 1960. In March 1960 Nyerere held talks in Britain to arrange for internal self-government. During these talks he insisted on full independence during 1961. In the September 1960 elections TANU won all but one seat and Tanzania became independent in December 1961. TANU later changed its name to Chama Cha Mapinduzi.

Independent Tanzania's economy is predominantly agrarian, based on small family farms. It is the biggest employer of the country's labour force. It constitutes 50 per cent of the Gross Domestic Product and more than 70 per cent of foreign exchange earnings accrued from this sector. Ninety per cent of food consumed in Tanzania is produced in the country. Agricultural producers can be divided as follows: peasant farmers, who cultivate up to ten hectares of land; medium and large-scale commercial farmers, who have between ten and a hundred hectares; and estates which mainly grow commercial crops such as coffee, cotton, sisal, cashew nuts, tobacco, tea, pyrethrum, seed, beans and wheat. Small farmers contribute the biggest share (85 per cent) in growth of these crops.

Since agriculture plays such an important role, the government has placed great emphasis on the development of rural areas. This emphasis had to be translated into action within the context of an overall development strategy. The now famous Arusha Declaration of 1967 spelt out such a development strategy. Pursuant to this Declaration, socialism and self-reliance became the cornerstones of Tanzania's political philosophy. Stress was placed on equality and development through utilization of four major resources: people, land, sound policies and sound leadership. Four basic principles guided the implementation of this strategy, namely: public ownership of the major means of production, absence of exploitation of man by man, democracy, and human (sexual) equality.

It was decided that the best manner of implementing this strategy was to resettle peasant families in Ujamaa villages to which basic social services – such as water, health, education, agricultural inputs – could be more easily distributed. Resettlement took off rather slowly but accelerated in the 1970s. Thus by 1982, 8,299 such villages, accommodating approximately 85 per cent of the rural population, were in existence. While most such villages are neither traditional nor Ujamaa (communal) settlements, the ultimate goal is to transform them into fully communal ones where people live together, own and control all major means of production jointly, and where all members have equal rights. In the village each adult must be provided with land which he or she must cultivate to produce both food and commercial crops. The proceeds accruing from the land belong to the individual producers. Each member also has to contribute to the communal economic activities of the village. The proceeds from these activities are controlled by the Village Government. A portion of the proceeds is retained for the village development projects and to sustain social services. The rest is distributed to villagers according to individual contributions.

Women have benefited greatly from the "villagization" programme, in that they now have relatively easy access to clean water, medical services, educational facilities, etc. Furthermore, they are for the first time being paid directly and independently for their labour.

The Village Governments were established by virtue of the Villages Act of 1975, vested with full legal powers. Each registered village had to have a 25-member elected Village Council, with five committees of five people each and a Village Assembly, composed of all adult village members, which is the final decision-making body. The five committees are finance and planning, construction and transport, education, culture and social welfare, security and defence, production and marketing. Each village is also meant to have a party branch as well as branches of various mass organizations like the women's organization UWT (Umoja wa Wanawake wa Tanganyika.)

Tanzania's industrial sector is at an elementary stage, though there has been gradual expansion since independence. Its main activities centre on the processing of agricultural goods and the assembling of machinery whose parts are usually imported. Only 6 per cent of adults are employed within the industrial sector. While it is the desire of the government to promote basic industries, such as the paper and chemical industries as well as iron and steel manufacturing, it is faced with many problems. These include low productivity and the shortage of foreign exchange for the importation of raw materials and spares. In the support sector, difficulties such as frequent interruptions and insufficient supplies of power, coupled with the high cost of transport, compound the above problems.

At independence, only a quarter of Tanzania's population was literate. Recognizing that illiteracy is a major obstacle to development, the ruling party and the government placed great emphasis on education and ensured that most Tanzanian children had access to schools. Although the country's population has almost doubled since independence, the literacy rate is now 85 per cent.

Women in Tanzania

Due to the absence of research regarding women in Tanzania before European occupation, very little is known about them. What is clear, however, is that matrilineal societies existed in Tanzania as in other parts of Africa during this period. Some survived European colonization. Islamic influence which is patriarchal, particularly on the island of Zanzibar (which constitutes a part of the United Republic of Tanzania) significantly weakened the position of the Tanzanian woman. Similarly Christianity, also very patriarchal in its beliefs and practices, contributed much to the lowering of the status of women in mainland Tanzania.

The colonizing Germans and British, when introducing

214

cash crop farming in Tanzania, completely ignored the essential role that women played in the agricultural sector and did not utilize their skill and labour. They transformed it into an exclusively male function. With the introduction of Western education by Europeans, girls did not have equal access to education.

TANU, aware of the disadvantages suffered by women, had to attend to the problems they gave rise to. In 1954 when a draft constitution for the forerunner of TANU was prepared, provision was made for a women's section. During its mobilization of the people to campaign for independence, TANU enrolled thousands of women. A particularly active and effective organizer during this period was Bibi Titi Mohamed, a Matumbi woman. She recruited Dar-es-Salaam's women brewers and campaigned house-to-house, winning villagers' support not only for political independence but also for the equal participation of women in society. She formed the first women's section in 1955.

The position of women in Tanzania has been improved since independence. In the resettled villages, many rural women now have relatively easy access to clean water, medical services and educational facilities. In these Ujamaa villages (the structure of which is explained earlier on) women for the first time are being paid directly and independently for their labour input.

Men and women are equal before the law. Women have the right to vote and contest for elections. Married women have the same rights as men to acquire, hold and dispose of property whether movable or immovable and the same rights regarding contracts.

The Villages Act of 1975, setting up Village Governments, has facilitated women's involvement in decision-making. Although few women hold leadership positions at village level, the Committees are an infrastructure which easily facilitates their involvement in decision-making at the grassroots level. The Act, together with "villagization", has smoothed the way for the formation of women's groups, usually under the supervision of community development officers and the UWT. Women attend village meetings and express their opinions openly and freely.

At a national level there is one female member of the Central Committee of the ruling party. The National Executive has several women members and three women are Members of Parliament and ministers. The UWT has played a significant role in bringing about changes in the status of women and campaigning for the total reintegration of women in all aspects of Tanzanian society. It campaigned successfully for the introduction of maternity leave regulations which provide for security of tenure and a portion of their salary during confinement for mothers, regardless of their marital status. Also, girls are allowed direct entry to university after high school, instead of going to work for two years as is the national requirement. The UWT has further established many day-care centres.

The efforts which have been put into allowing girls easier access to education, including technical education, has resulted in a steady increase in their enrolment. Female enrolment for all forms stood at 30.3 per cent in 1978 and rose to 32 per cent in 1983. Enrolment of girls in technical secondary schools began after 1976 and a special quota was designated.

As so many problems remain, women have continued to request, through the UWT, that steps be taken to redress the current imbalance existing between the sexes. They have asked, among other things, for Family Life Education in schools, Adult Education Centres, where women who could not finish their schooling could go, and positive discrimination in favour of women, together with remedial measures in as many areas as is necessary.

The Role of Women in the Liberation Struggle and Reconstruction: Tanzanian Experience*

ZUKY N. MIHYO & LETTICIA RUTASHOBYA

The issue of the role of women in the liberation struggle and their participation in national reconstruction, either after a liberation war or in countries which achieved national independence without a full-scale liberation war, is gaining serious attention at present. This attention is both necessary and warranted, since various issues pertain to the subject, which require theoretical clarification and political self-inspection in terms of how the question as a whole is being tackled by national liberation movements engaged in continuing struggles; popular movements in countries that have recently attained national independence following liberation wars, and in independent states attempting to channel the energies of their mass nationalist organizations into resolving various aspects of the national liberation question.

The question of women's emancipation cannot be separated from the role of women in liberation struggles, and their participation in national reconstruction after independence, if one understands clearly the roots of exploitation and oppression which themselves lead to the common outcry - emancipation!

* This paper was delivered at a Women's Forum organized by the Pan Africanist Congress of Azania held in Dar-es-Salaam in July 1980. The theme was "Women in the Liberation Struggle".

The fundamental question asked by Machel[1] and which we have to ask ourselves is, how can one make a revolution or struggle without mobilizing women? If more than half of the exploited and oppressed people consist of women, how can they be left on the fringe of the struggle? To organize a liberation struggle it is necessary to mobilize all the exploited and oppressed, and consequently women as well. This is so because women are part of the society which is, itself, being exploited by another group. Thus, we cannot talk of women's emancipation without referring to the exploitation of the society as a whole. This is why many people tend to ignore the primary contradiction and subsequently take the secondary ones, which usually arise between men and women, as a kind of reflex of the primary one. The enemy would very much encourage such divisions, which in the final analysis weaken the struggle against the main enemy – imperialism.

From the above view, therefore, it will be found that the question of women's liberation is an historical one and has to be analysed critically, starting with the period before the coming of colonialism; then through the colonial period, up to the period after independence. This historical analysis will go hand in hand with the examination of the position occupied by women in Tanzanian society since pre-colonial times up to the present.

Pre-Colonial Period

Women have often been regarded as inferior to men in many societies. For instance, in the Holy Bible it is said that men were the first people to be created and that women were created out of a man's left ribs. Such is the basis of many people's belief that women are inferior to men.

The fact that women differ from men physiologically should not be used as a justification for treating women as second-class citizens. A scientific analysis of societies from primitive communalism to the post-colonial period will show that, up to a certain stage in the human history, women are not considered inferior to their male counterparts.

Tanzania passed through various stages during its pre-colonial period. Primitive communalism was the dominant mode of production in most places and feudalism in the rest. The basis of production was the household and people produced only enough to subsist. Property and land were communally owned; both men and women joined together and fought Nature with primitive tools. It is obvious, therefore, that there was a limited surplus economy because of the primitive methods employed in the production process. Technological advancement, which brought increased production, took ground later. At this stage, people started to produce more than they consumed – i.e. *surplus product was realized*, thus laying the material foundations for the emergence of a stratum in society which would appropriate the products of the masses' labour power. This is the essence of the system of exploitation of man by man and the core of the antagonistic relations which have divided society for years. Women were, therefore, part of the exploited group. But women as reproducers and as workers suffered more. As cited before, land came into private hands through the use of organized combat forces. Women, being generally less physically endowed for the use of single weapons, generally established no rights over land. Control over land necessitated control over labour, hence the control over women by men as labourers and reproducers of the labour force. With regard to this view, Samora Machel argues:

> To possess women is to possess workers, unpaid workers, workers whose entire labour power can be appropriated without resistance, by the husband, who is the lord and master.[2]

Therefore, in an agrarian economy, marrying more women is a sure way of accumulating a great deal of wealth. This is the important role played by polygamy in the rural areas with such an economy.

Colonial Period

Colonialism essentially means domination of one nation by another, politically, economically, socially and culturally. Colonialism came about when, in the early stages of industrialization, the European mercantile groups, either on their own or working for their kings and churches, travelled to the continents of the south – Asia, Africa and the Americas – to seek industrial raw materials such as dyes, spices, timber, minerals and tropical fruits. These were acquired through both trade and plunder. Once the impact of these goods on European economies became evident, an all-out scramble ensued whereby European powers fought the dwellers of other countries and each other to occupy and rule territories they perceived as being rich in the resources that were in demand at the time. The period also ushered in the second era of slavery, which provided cheap labour for colonial settlers to mine the ground, to harvest the timber or to cultivate cash crops, particularly sugar, tea and coffee.

The vast amount of wealth accumulated in this manner accelerated industry and productivity in Europe and led to the rise of a new force, the industrialists and investors, who may not have been the holders of any feudal titles but who became very influential as their collective wealth began to surpass that of royalty and nobility. Thus, the capitalist class harnessed productive forces so great that the best placed established monopolies which transcended national boundaries. They exported capital to whichever territories promised higher returns and developed into what we now know as international monopoly finance capitalists, or modern imperialists, as Marx and Lenin designated them.

Spheres of influences were immediately established in order to initiate and perpetuate the process of exploitation in Third World countries. Hence Tanzania also found itself within the web of imperialist manoeuvres. Pre-capitalist social formations were destroyed, although some of them that were considered useful by the colonialists were conserved or preserved – the conservation-destruction process being the first step towards the perfection of the colonial rule.

Colonialism, with its characteristic cash-crop production, increased the burden for Tanzanian women. Crops were sold to the colonial state, which then exported them to the mother countries. Moreover, the colonial state introduced what were called hut-tax and poll-tax, to be paid by every able-bodied Tanzanian above the age of 18. Therefore, men were forced to work in European-owned plantations. In so doing they were paid in cash, which made it possible for them to pay these taxes. Men were, thus, separated from their women because they had to migrate to areas where these plantations were established. The Tanzanian men worked in the plantations on a seasonal basis, and in most cases were migrant and not permanent labourers and so were paid less than the value of their labour power. This enabled the colonialists to realize generous surplus value in the form of profit. Surplus value was created from the sweat of Tanzanian men – i.e. unpaid labour power or undistributed wages.

Other Tanzanians worked in colonial offices as messengers, clerks and sweepers; some were teachers and policemen. All of them were paid less than the value of their labour. Most political economists recognize this as the ultimate source of profit, the value that arises after the calculation of all production costs and wages. Its source can only be the unpaid part of the value of workers' wages. Thus we can see that colonialism brought misery and suffering for the majority of the Tanzanian population.

Women, on the other hand, stayed at home working on the farms and taking care of the children, the old and the sick; in short, men were mainly involved in the cash economy while the women were engaged in the subsistence and domestic economy. The women were forced to work even harder in order to supplement their husbands' meagre incomes. Apart from farm work, women also had to attend to other household chores such as cooking, washing, cleaning the house and the surroundings, fetching water, collecting firewood and sometimes tending cattle and goats.

At this juncture, therefore, both men and women were confronted with a common enemy, the colonizer; but, as said before, a woman was not as free as a man because of his mobility and earning power. She was doubly exploited and hence doubly oppressed and held the lowest position in society.

When we analyse the second part of the colonial period, that is during the struggle for independence, the woman's story in Tanzania takes on a different shape. The woman who was oppressed and humiliated did not hesitate to support her male counterpart in the struggle for independence, because Tanzanian women knew that the only possible solution to the woman question was social emancipation – liberation of the exploited masses from colonialism and all its manifestations. The liberation of the society at large was the first step towards the liberation of women. You cannot talk of emancipating women from men's oppression while their entire community is a subjugated one. It is by solving the principal and major contradication that the secondary contradictions can be solved.

So, Tanzanian women joined hands with their menfolk to fight that great monster the colonizer. It is true that very few women participated in the nationalist struggle in Tanzania, but their role cannot be underestimated. The part they played was significant because it showed that humanity rejects any form of oppression. Women participated actively in political rallies organized by the then political party TANU. They also organized campaigns for the party. They did not disclose members of the party who were being hunted by the colonial state like criminals. In this way Tanzanian women managed to show their men that, although they were being looked upon as inferior, they could cope with the essential tasks of the nationalist struggle. Such women included Ndugu Lucy Lameck and Ndugu Bibi Titi.

When independence was finally attained, social equality was legally recognized by the TANU government, as was stipulated in the party's constitution. It stated, in part, that "every individual has the right to receive a just return of his labour" and that the main aim of the party was "to see that the government gives equal opportunity to all men and women irrespective of race, religion, or status".[2]

In 1962 the Union of Women of Tanzania (UWT) was formed. It is the sole organization which caters for the interests of Tanzanian women. The objectives of UWT are many, the major one is to see that women restore the dignity they deserve as human beings. UWT has done a lot to try to solve women's problems, although with less success because of various shortcomings which will also be mentioned.

The second main objective of UWT is to instil in Tanzanian women a political consciousness which ties with our ideology of Ujamaa and Self-Reliance – that is living together and working together for the benefit of the whole nation; moreover, UWT encourages co-operative endeavours among women so as to establish productive projects for the benefit of all Tanzanian women as a whole and the society in general. Therefore, various projects have been launched by UWT, and the ruling party, Chama Cha Mapinduzi gives subsidies to some projects.

Types of Projects Undertaken by UWT

(a) Education-Oriented Projects

These include seminars organized by UWT, which give lessons on various subjects such as nutrition, sewing, gardening, poultry-keeping. The women here are taught these lessons so that they become independent, by making simple clothes for themselves and their children. For example they are also taught how to prepare a balanced diet. Home economics and family planning lessons are undertaken together with literacy classes.

(b) Economic Projects

These types of projects include those activities which are done on a co-operative basis and generate some money for the members – e.g. handcrafts, such as the making of mats, embroidery, baskets, pots etc. They also include tailoring and poultry farming.

(c) Service-Giving Projects

Service-oriented projects are those concerned with providing services to the society at large and women and children in particular. Such activities include the running of day-care centres and the provision of ante-natal services and clinics for the young children. However, all these projects as seen on the surface are very good in that if successfully carried out they can benefit the whole society. Therefore, UWT has tried to make sure that many of its objectives succeed though there are bottlenecks. UWT is and can be a very useful tool for the emancipation of women but at present it has problems which have made some of its objectives mere illusions.

First, the majority of UWT members had minimum education, i.e. below standard seven. This is so because of our historical background; traditionally our fathers and forefathers preferred to educate male children because they considered educating female children as useless. Therefore, we find in Tanzania that there are very few educated women, and this is exacerbated by the fact that UWT has very few branches in colleges and secondary schools.

Second, there is this misconception of "women's lib" – which essentially means liberating women from oppression and exploitation of any kind, and that a woman has to be considered equal to her male counterpart, and hence she too has to take part in all activities done by men and be paid justly. Women's "lib" does not simply mean the sharing or exchanging of household duties. In the words of Samora Machel, women's "lib" should not be mechanically interpreted i.e, mechanically dividing their household chores: "If I wash the dishes today you must wash them tomorrow, whether or not you are busy or have time." Women's "lib" is not as mechanical as other people think.

Women's emancipation requires action on several essential levels. First, women must be politically conscious and committed in order to be able to undertake this great task of emancipating the exploited and oppressed masses in general and women in particular. That is why at the beginning we pointed out that, during the liberation struggle, the struggle between men and women must be kept in the background, and the major contradiction, in other words the struggle of the colonized people against the colonizer must come to the fore. This is necessarily so because during this period the relationship between men and women has to appear not as sex relations but as social relations. However, there are particular relations in different societies depending on concrete situations. Therefore, action should be taken appropriate to each situation. For example, Tanzania's situation during colonial times was different from that of either Kenya or Mozambique, likewise the present Azanian case. In this way the woman question has to be examined differently in different societies depending on specific conditions pertaining to those societies. At present efforts of both women and men should be concentrated on the main contradiction, that is of ousting the colonizer and the imperialist.

NOTES

1. Samora Moises Machel, late president of Mozambique, in *Sowing the Seeds of Revolution*, a compilation of his speeches published by Mozambique's ruling party.
2. Ibid.

VII: Lesotho, Malawi, Swaziland, Zambia

Lesotho

The most obvious feature about Lesotho is the fact that it is completely surrounded by South Africa. It has borders with three South African provinces, Natal, the Orange Free State and the Cape Province. It has an area of 30,355 square kilometres and two thirds of the country consists of mountains.

The founding father of the modern Basotho nation was King Moshoeshoe who was born around 1786. He moulded his nation from refugees of wars with other ethnic groups in the region, in the main those under the military and political leadership of King Shaka. Later on, faced with hostility from and invasions by the Dutch colonists (Boers) King Moshoeshoe chose what seemed at the time the better of two evils and negotiated with the British administration in the Cape Colony for "protection". Lesotho became a crown colony in 1884. It became independent from Britain on 4 October 1966.

Its unfortunate geographical position has made Lesotho much more vulnerable to the manipulations of the regime in South Africa than other independent states in the region. This was illustrated in January 1986 when, displeased about the Prime Minister's refusal to sign a "peace" treaty with them, the South Africans refused to allow any goods to pass through to Lesotho. A military coup followed days after the economic blockade and the latter was lifted immediately thereafter.

Approximately fifteen thousand Basotho men work in the mines of South Africa. In those instances women have to take sole responsibility for the maintenance of the family and farming. Maize, sorghum, wheat, peas, beans and barley are grown.

The problems experienced by women elsewhere in the

region, particularly in the rural areas, such as long hours and strenuous manual work are also experienced by women in Lesotho. On the positive side Lesotho has one of the highest female literacy rates on the continent. Girls outnumber boys in school attendance, one of the reasons being that boys are often kept or taken out of school to be herdsmen.

In 1979 the government set up the Lesotho Women's Bureau in the Office of the Prime Minister. It has subsequently been moved to the Ministry of Rural Development, Co-operatives and Women's Affairs. One of its most important objectives is to develop a policy for women in harmony with national development policies. It has the task of co-ordinating women's organizations in the country, women's projects and training programmes. It also monitors and evaluates projects involving women.

Malawi

Malawi is situated in the south-eastern part of Africa. It has a total area of 118,484 square kilometres and is bordered by Tanzania, Mozambique and Zambia.

Sophisticated states and centralized systems of government prevailed in what is now central and southern Malawi, and reached their zenith in the seventeenth century and affected surrounding areas in what is now Zambia and Mozambique. The slave trade in the late eighteenth century and British colonialism in the late nineteenth century disrupted much of this. Between 1951 and 1953 the British decided, despite opposition from Africans, to join Southern and Northern Rhodesia and Nyasaland into a federation. The federation was dissolved in 1963 and Malawi became independent in 1964, with Hastings Kamuzu Banda as President. He was made president for life in 1971.

Malawi is the only country on the continent which is not a member of the Organization of African Unity. It is also the only African country which has diplomatic relations with the white South African government.

Malawi's economy is largely dependent on agriculture. About 95 per cent of its exports are derived from agriculture. Most important among these are tobacco, tea, sugar and peanuts. Subsistence agriculture forms a significant section, although cash crop farming is on the increase.

The national representative body of women in Malawi is the League of Malawi Women. The latter body has contributed to the alleviation of some of the problems experienced by women in the country. In 1984 the Malawi National Commission on Women was established. The Commission functions as a coordinator and catalyst and is not in itself responsible for the implementation of programmes. This is left for individual ministries, parastatals and non-governmental organizations. The Commission's work is carried out by what is termed subject-matter committees, which include education and training committees; family health and welfare; planning, research and evaluation; small- and medium-scale enterprises; women and employment; women in society: women and agriculture; and a legal committee. Each committee is chaired by a ministry or non-governmental organization that has expertise in the given subject area. Each subject has clearly defined terms of reference. While this is a step in the right direction it cannot be effective until its objectives are translated into practice. The fact that at present the Commission has no budget of its own must affect its ability to make this possible.

Swaziland

Swaziland has a total land area of 17,364 square kilometres and is situated between South Africa to the north, west and south and Mozambique to the east. The country is rich in agricultural land and mineral resources. Nine-tenths of the population is engaged in subsistence farming, with women traditionally playing an important role. Rice and fruits such as bananas and oranges are grown under irrigation, while maize, cotton, beans, tobacco and pineapples are raised on dry ground. The country's main exports are wood-pulp and iron-ore. All mining operations are foreign-controlled.

Swaziland, like Botswana and Lesotho, was a British protectorate. It became independent in 1968 with King Sobhuza II at its helm. In 1973 the King dismissed the British-designed constitution and reinstated the more ancient system of Swazi government. Two of the most important features of this system are the type of land ownership and the role of the royal family. All land belongs to the Swazi nation as a whole and is vested in the King in trust. All political power is vested in the King who, in exercising it, is advised by the Council of State or Liqoqo. The King appoints the Prime Minister and a Cabinet, remnants of the British-designed constitution. The young Prince Makhosetive was crowned King Mswati III in early 1986, after the death of his father in 1982.

Swazi women have traditionally played an important role in the political and agricultural life of their people. They are responsible (with some assistance from men) for the cultivation of crops. During summer they leave their homes in the villages and stay near the fields for this purpose. Recognition of this role has not been forthcoming and discrimination is common. Women experience problems in obtaining credit without the permission of their husbands, who are often away in the mines of South Africa, since Swaziland remains a major source of migrant male labour.

Zambia

Zambia is situated in south central Africa. It stretches over an area of 752,614 square kilometres and is landlocked. It has borders with Angola, Zaïre, Tanzania, Malawi, Mozambique, Zimbabwe, Botswana and a small strip of land from Namibia called the Caprivi Strip. Formerly known as Northern Rhodesia, Zambia became independent on 24 October 1964. The United National Independence Party (UNIP) spearheaded resistance to British colonialism and became the ruling party at independence.

Zambia's economy has been largely dependent on the mining and export of copper. The sharp fall in the copper prices since 1975 has adversely affected the economy. The closure of the border during the war in Zimbabwe and the civil war in Angola further contributed to an economic crisis from which Zambia has not yet recovered. Attempts have been made to diversify the economy, although dependence on copper continues. About 65 per cent of the people of Zambia derive a living directly from agriculture. Maize, sugar, tobacco, cotton, coffee, fruit and vegetables are grown.

Although women constitute slightly more than half the population, only 24.2 per cent were considered economically active in the formal sector in 1979. This is obviously a gross under-utilization of the country's human resources. Women also have a disproportionately higher rate of illiteracy.

The Women's Bureau is the official organization of women in Zambia. It is located within the structure of UNIP and falls under the Women's Affairs Committee of the Central Committee. It is responsible for the formulation of policies on women, particularly those which would encourage their effective integration in development. The Women's League, a mass umbrella organization, is responsible for the implementation of national policies concerning women. It operates at all levels of the party structure. Both the Women's Affairs Committee and the Women's League are headed by women who are also members of UNIP's Central Committee. This should ensure that the concerns of women are voiced at the highest party level. Problems remain, however. While noteworthy decisions are taken they often do not get implemented because of the inadequate structure and machinery. Lack of data and information on the situation of women which is necessary for proper planning and programming is also a major drawback.

Conclusion

For the achievements and the successes of the women past and present, enumerated in the collection, we must render due praise. Regarding the difficulties faced by them, I would like to suggest that the measures listed below will assist their reintegration into society at all levels.

Research

The solution of any problem can only be effected after proper analysis of that problem. Those relating to women are no exception. Those responsible for the collection of data must ensure that it is done by skilled persons familiar with the social, political and cultural milieu of the women. Other effective ways of gathering information are discussion groups and workshops where women feel free to air their views. Not only problems but also their practical solutions should be solicited as this will facilitate the implementation of any measures taken in pursuance of such investigations.

The concerns of women in the region should be seen as of such vital importance that in the next few years it should become part of every country's national development plan. A first step in this direction has been taken by women from the region. As of August 1986 proposals (which seemed certain to be accepted) for the establishment of a Women in Development Sector within SADCC structures were being drafted. In practical terms, this will ensure that at every meeting of SADCC, whatever decisions are taken, the concerns of women will have to be taken into account.

Agriculture

The discrepancy between the contribution of women to this sector on the one hand and practical recognition and assistance on the other is a major obstacle to food self-sufficiency in most countries. It has been seen in Zimbabwe what can be achieved with access to credit facilities and technical advice to subsistence and small-scale farmers. If this strategy could be employed with women farmers, countries would be spared the humiliation of having to receive food aid from outside Africa. Even where natural disasters occur, the effect would not be so devastating.

In Southern Africa much of, and in some countries all, commercial banking is foreign-owned and controlled. As far as these institutions are concerned, female farmers are invisible and inconsequential. Governments which have not already done so, should intervene and create state lending institutions with special credit divisions for women. Alternatively, they should exert pressure on foreign-controlled bankers to change their policies vis à vis women. Kenya scored a notable first with the establishment of the first bank in the world managed and run by women to deal exclusively with women clients.

More female extension workers and agricultural advisers should be recruited and trained so as to deal with the problem of prejudiced male advisers.

Appropriate Technology

The substitution of wood as the main source of energy in rural areas is essential. It will lessen the workload of the rural woman who often has to walk long distances carrying heavy loads. It will also help to halt the desertification brought about by the continual cutting of trees. Innovations, such as the sheet metal stoves introduced in Botswana, for instance, which substantially reduce the amount of wood needed, should now be considered a priority.

The availability and transportation of water should receive the attention of policy-makers, whose brief should be to lessen the time rural women spend on the procurement of water.

Literacy

Non-governmental organizations, no matter how well intentioned, cannot take responsibility for this all-important task. This should rest with the various governments. The successful implementation of other measures does to a large extent depend on the rate of literacy. Illiteracy in most societies is more prevalent among women. Creative and stimulating approaches to literacy advancement can be tied to problem-solving and community mobilization. Brazilian educationalist Paulo Freire has evolved a dynamic literacy method which is based on discussion with and involvement of participants. It has the added advantage of socializing participants into self-expression.

Legislation and Education

Legislation, while not in itself enough, must nevertheless be enacted to safeguard women from ill-treatment and discrimination in the workplace, educational institutions and even in the home. Laws which discriminate against women relating to marriage, inheritance and custody of children must be reviewed as they cause much hardship.

Wide-ranging education campaigns, aimed at both men and women, which will provoke discussion and debate on women's roles, health matters, cultural domination and alienation, should be instituted. To be thorough they should take place at village, district and town level.

At a personal level, the biological need to nurture the young and social reality places women in a position to make profound and lasting impressions on the minds and attitudes of their children. This gives them an opportunity to inculcate positive values in them, especially the girls. It would mean, for instance, that instead of preparing girls to become only nurses, teachers, wives and mothers, they should be given the option of becoming engineers, horticulturists and technicians.

In Namibia and Azania the essential first step of dismantling the colonial state apparatus must be accelerated. In the interim women should be organized, through both the liberation movement and independent women's organizations, in order that they may at independence take their rightful place next to their male compatriots in the rebuilding of their societies.

These suggestions are by no means original. They have been made previously, often in more detail. It is necessary, however, that they be repeated as often as possible until they are implemented. Some have been accepted in principle and others implemented in some countries in the region. Zimbabwe, since independence in 1980, has made a good start in the direction of these goals and it is hoped that they will continue in this vein and so set an example which will inspire others within and outside of Africa.

Whatever else is said or done, women themselves are going to have to take major responsibility for the restoration of their human worth and authority.

Glossary

Azania – The African name for South Africa.

Frontline States – A grouping of Southern African states which meet regularly to co-ordinate policy decisions and action regarding the liberation struggle in Namibia and Azania, aggression from South Africa and other issues affecting the region. It came into being in February 1976 in order to deal with the Zimbabwean struggle. Its decisions are often used as a guide for action by other African countries as well as countries abroad. The members are Tanzania, Botswana, Zimbabwe, Zambia, Mozambique and Angola.

Namibia – The African name for South West Africa.

Organization of African Unity (OAU) – The organization was founded in Addis Ababa, Ethiopia, in 1963. The main driving force behind its formation was Kwame Nkrumah of Ghana; he, Sékou Touré of Guinea and Haile Selassie of Ethiopia became its founding fathers. Its objective was to promote continental unity and co-operation. One of its most important achievements has been its contribution to the decolonization of Southern Africa. All countries on the continent with the exception of Malawi and of course South Africa and South West Africa are members of the OAU.

Southern African Development Co-ordination Conference (SADCC) – An association of nine politically independent states in Southern Africa: Tanzania, Botswana, Zimbabwe, Lesotho, Malawi, Mozambique, Swaziland, Angola and Zambia. Founded in 1980, SADCC's stated objectives are the reduction of economic dependence, particularly, but not only, on South Africa; the forging of links to create a genuine and equitable regional integration, the mobilization of resources to promote the implementation of national, interstate and regional policies.

Women's Organizations in Southern Africa

AZANIA
African National Congress (ANC) Women's Section
P.O. Box 31791
Lusaka
Zambia

Pan Africanist Congress of Azania (PAC) Women's Wing
P.O. Box 2412
Dar-es-Salaam
Tanzania

Black Women's Economic Development Association (BWEDA)
P.O. Box 3419
North-End
Port Elizabeth
South Africa

Black Women Unite (BWU)
Letkon House
Wanderers Street
Johannesburg
South Africa

BOTSWANA
Botswana Council of Women (BCW)
P.O. Box 339
Gaborone

Botswana Women's Affairs Unit
Ministry of Labour and Home Affairs
Private Bag 002
Gaborone

Young Women's Christian Association (YWCA)
P.O. Box 359
Gaborone

LESOTHO
Lesotho Women's Bureau
Ministry of Rural Development, Cooperatives and Women's Affairs
P.O. Box 686
Maseru

Lesotho National Council of Women
P.O. Box 686
Maseru
Lesotho

MALAWI
The League of Malawi Women
Ministry of Community Services
Private Bag 330
Lilongwe

NAMIBIA
South West Africa People's Organization (SWAPO)
    Women's Council
P.O. Box 30577
Lusaka
Zambia

SWAZILAND
Umbrella Women's Organization
Ministry of Foreign Affairs
P.O. Box 518
Mbabane

TANZANIA
Union of Women of Tanzania (UWT)
P.O. Box 1473
Dar-es-Salaam

ZAMBIA
The Women's League
P.O. Box 30302
Lusaka

Women's Affairs Committee
P.O. Box 30302
Lusaka

ZIMBABWE
Ministry of Community Development and Women's Affairs
Private Bag 7735
Causeway
Harare

Association of Women's Clubs
64 Selous Avenue
7th Street
Harare

Select Bibliography

Aldred, Cyril, *Jewels of the Pharaohs* (London: Thames and Hudson, 1971).

Biko, Steve, *I Write What I Like*, ed. Aelred Stubbs (London: Heinemann, 1980).

Boserup, Ester, *Women's Role in Economic Development* (London: Allen & Unwin, 1970).

Davidson, Basil, *Africa – History of a Continent* (New York: Macmillan, 1972).

Davis, Angela, *Women, Race and Class* (New York: Vintage Books, 1983).

Diop, Cheikh Anta, *The African Origin of Civilization* (Westport, Conn.: Lawrence Hill & Co., 1974).

Diop, Cheikh Anta, *Black Africa: The Economic and Cultural Basis for a Federated State* (Westport, Conn.: Lawrence Hill & Co., 1974).

Diop, Cheikh Anta, *The Cultural Unity of Black Africa* (Chicago: Third World Press, 1978).

Emecheta, Buchi, and Maggie Murray, *Our Own Freedom* (London: Sheba, 1981).

Fanon, Frantz, *A Dying Colonialism* (London: Writers and Readers Publishing Cooperative, 1980).

Garlake, Peter, *The Kingdoms of Africa* (Oxford: Elsevier, 1978).

Harding, Vincent, *There is a River: The Black Struggle for Freedom in America* (New York: Harcourt Brace Jovanovich, 1981).

Houston, Druscilla Dunjee, *Wonderful Ethiopians of the Ancient Cushite Empire* (Baltimore: Black Classic Press, 1985).

Iliffe, John, *A Modern History of Tanganyika* (Cambridge: Cambridge University Press, 1979).

Isaacmen, Stephen and Barbara, *Mozambique: Women, the Law and Agrarian Reform* (1980).

Jackson, John G., *Introduction to African Civilizations* (New Jersey: Citadel Press, 1970).

Kahn *et al.*, *From Protest to Challenge* (California: Sheridan Johns, 1972).

Kimble, Judy, *et al.*, *"We Opened the Road for You, You Must Go Forward"*, ANC Women's Struggles 1912–1982.

Ki-Zerbo, J. (ed.), *Unesco General History of Africa*, Vol. 1 (London:

Heinemann/Berkeley: University of California, 1981).

Kuper, Hilda, *An African Aristocracy* (Oxford: Oxford University Press, 1969).

Kuzwayo, Ellen, *Call Me Woman* (London: Women's Press, 1985).

Leland, Stephanie, Joyce Mutasa and Fran Willard, *Women of Southern Africa: Struggles and Achievements – The UN Decade for Women Diary July 1985/86* (London: Feminist International for Peace and Food, 1985).

Madhubuti, Haki R., *Enemies: The Clash of Races* (Chicago: Third World Press, 1978).

Martin, David, and Phyllis Johnson, *The Struggle for Zimbabwe* (Harare: Zimbabwe Publishing House, 1981).

Marx, Karl, and Frederick Engels, *Selected Works*, Vol. 3 (Moscow: Progress Publishers, 1970).

Mokgethi, Motlhabi, *The Theory and Practice of Black Resistance to Apartheid* (Johannesburg: Skotaville, 1984).

Muchena, Olivia N., *Women's Organizations in Zimbabwe: An Assessment of their Needs, Achievement and Potential* (Harare: University of Zimbabwe, 1980).

Mutunhu, Tendai, "Nehanda of Zimbabwe", in *Ufahamu* (National Archives, Harare, Zimbabwe).

Pheko, Motsoko, *The Story of a Dispossessed People* (London: Marram Books, 1984).

Omer-Cooper, J.D., *The Zulu Aftermath* (London: Longman, 1966).

Ranger, Terence O., *Revolt in Southern Rhodesia 1867-70* (London: Heinemann, 1967).

Reynolds, Edward, *Stand the Storm: A History of the Atlantic Slave Trade* (London/New York: Allison & Busby, 1985).

Rodney, Walter, *How Europe Underdeveloped Africa* (London: Bogle-L'Ouverture Publications, 1972; Washington: Howard University Press).

Rout, Leslie B., Jr, *The African Experience in Spanish America* (Cambridge: Cambridge University Press, 1976).

Sached Trust, *Working Women: A Portrait of South Africa's Black Women Workers* (Johannesburg: Ravan Press, 1985).

Schipper, Mineke (ed.), *Unheard Words: Women and Literature in Africa, the Arab World, Asia, the Caribbean and Latin America* (London/New York: Allison & Busby, 1984).

Sweetman, David, *Women Leaders in African History* (London: Heinemann Educational Books, 1984).

Tsele, Lindiwe M., *Zimbabwe Women in Chimurenga* (London: Black Women's Centre, 1981).

Tlou, Thomas, and Alec Campbell, *History of Botswana* (Macmillan, 1984).

Urdang, Stephanie, *Fighting Two Colonialisms: Women in Guinea-Bissau* (New York: Monthly Review Press, 1979).

Van Sertima, Ivan (ed.), *Blacks in Science: Ancient and Modern* (New Brunswick: Transaction Books, 1983).

Van Sertima, Ivan (ed.), *Black Women in Antiquity* (New Brunswick: Transaction Books, 1985).

Williams, Chancellor, *The Destruction of Black Civilization* (Chicago: Third World Press, 1976).

About the Contributors

Nomvo Booi is currently a member of the Central Committee of the Pan-Africanist Congress of Azania (PAC), having been involved with this movement since its origins in 1959, when it developed out of the Youth League of the African National Congress (ANC). She has been imprisoned numerous times because of her political activities.

Nora Chase, born in Windhoek in 1940, is Secretary for Foreign Affairs of the Politbureau of the South-West Africa National Union (SWANU) and is also Director of formal education with the Namibian Council of Churches.

Ruvimbo Chimedza is a lecturer in the Department of Adult Education at the University of Zimbabwe in Harare.

Zuky N. Mihyo obtained her Bachelor of Arts (BA) and Masters degrees in Dar es Salaam and the Netherlands respectively. She is lecturing in the Sociology Department of the University of Dar es Salaam, Tanzania.

Sibongile Mkhabela (née Mthembu) was the sole woman in the historic "Soweto 11" trial, involving the leaders of the Soweto Students Representative Council, after the June 1976 uprisings. She had already spent two years in police custody when she finally came to trial, at the age of twenty, in 1978, and after an eight-month case sentenced to four years imprisonment with two years of the sentence suspended. She was released in May 1981. She is a member of the Azanian People's Organization (AZAPO) and of Black Women Unite (BWU).

Olivia N. Muchena is a lecturer in the Department of Adult Education at the University of Zimbabwe in Harare.

Teurai Ropa Nhongo (née Mugari), now in her early thirties, is Minister of Community Development and Women's Affairs in the Zimbabwe government, having joined ZANU in 1973 during her country's liberation war.

Lesego Molapo is a commercial farmer, cattle breeder and horticulturalist in the Barolong area, one of Botswana's most productive regions. A primary school teacher by profession, she developed an interest in horticulture when asked to oversee the gardening at school. She resigned as a teacher in 1974 and became a full-time farmer (like her father). Until 1984, when she received financial assistance from the government, she had been struggling on her own with the support of her husband, who is not a farmer.

Margaret Nananyane Nasha, in her thirties, is the Director of the Department of Information and Broadcasting in Botswana, the second woman to occupy the post.

Dabi Nkululeko is an Azanian social scientist who is living in exile. She has written and delivered a number of essays dealing with the National Question in Azania at various forums, and is presently researching for a PhD on this topic in the United Kingdom and the University of Dar es Salaam, Tanzania.

Christine N. Qunta is an Azanian and was on the regional executive of the South African Students Organization (SASO) and Black People's Convention (BPC) in the 1970s. While doing active political work she was detained and forced to flee into exile. She completed a Law degree in Australia and is presently working as a solicitor in Botswana. She is the author of *Hoyi Na Azania – Poems of an African Struggle*.

Letticia Rutashobya, who has a BA and Masters degree in Marketing, lectures in the Faculty of Commerce and Management at the University of Dar es Salaam, Tanzania.

Ntomb'elanga Takawira (née Duhe) trained and worked as a nurse in Bulawayo, and in 1955 married Leopold Takawira, who was to become vice-president of ZANU (he died in prison in the then Rhodesia in 1970). Now in her fifties, she is a Zimbabwean senator.

Index